CREATING KIL

Also by Jean Robb and Hilary Letts

Creating Kids Who Can Concentrate
Creating Kids Who Can Pass Exams

Creating Kids
Who Can

Jean Robb and Hilary Letts

Illustrations by Penny Lovelock

HODDER

MOBIUS

Copyright © 1995 by Jean Robb and Hilary Letts

First published in 1995 by Hodder Headline Australia Pty Limited
First published in Great Britain in 1996
by Hodder and Stoughton
First published in paperback in 2002
by Hodder and Stoughton
A division of Hodder Headline

The right of Jean Robb and Hiliary Letts to be indentified as
the Authors of the Work has been asserted by them in
accordance with the Copyright, Designs and Patents Act 1988.

2 4 6 8 10 9 7 5 3 1

A CIP catalogue record for this title is available from the British
Library

ISBN 0 340 82043 8

Edited by Kate Tully
Designed by Liz Seymour

Printed and bound in Great Britain by
Mackays of Chatham plc, Chatham, Kent

Hodder and Stoughton
A division of Hodder Headline
338 Euston Road
London NW1 3BH

ABOUT THE AUTHORS

Jean Robb is an inspirational teacher. She has worked in many countries unravelling the mysteries of learning for parents and their children. Her holistic methods take away the barriers to learning that limit potential.

In 1990 she teamed up with children's librarian and teacher Hilary Letts to form the education foundation, Successful Learning.

As educational therapists, Jean and Hilary work with people who have barriers to learning. These include people who are very bright but disorganised; who have behavioural difficulties; who are wanting to overcome a weakness – academically or socially; who have suffered trauma; who have a physical difficulty or who need help in a particular subject. They also include people who don't know how to learn effectively; who panic; who have been labelled as having learning difficulties; who want to learn techniques for success in exams. Jean and Hilary also work with parents who have met a barrier when helping their children.

This book has grown out of more than 32 years experience in teaching children of every age and ability, and in dealing with their parents.

Now Jean and Hilary enable all children, even those labelled dull, lazy, naughty, difficult or remedial, to astound themselves and startle their teachers by making good the damage of years of missed leasons, misunderstood lessons and mixed messages.

Jean and Hilary also work with gifted children to liberate them from the stress of being superbright, especially gifted or multitalented, by showing them the way of realising their own potential, preventing them from becoming bored and allowing them to celebrate their gifts.

In addition to their work with children, Jean and Hilary also run courses for parents, adults with barriers to learning, and people who are experiencing stress, work difficulties or behavioural difficulties.

Jean and Hilary's practical tips are appreciated by readers of the parenting pages in the *Guardian* and in other publications for parents.

To Eve and Paddy and all those who care

To our families and friends who have listened,
questioned and challenged. To the parents and
children who have taught us to teach. To Angela
Anderson, Judith Edwards, Varlerie Clark,
Kate Tully and Philippa Sandall who have nurtured
us along, teaching us the skills we needed.

CONTENTS

INTRODUCTION

As parents, every new advance your child makes brings you a new delight, but it also brings you a new anxiety.

You feel so capable when your child seems to be learning: you can be at your wits' end when they are not.

You feel so relieved when things go well, but life never stands still – there is always something new to learn.

Few and far between are the parents who don't want to help their children, but common enough are those who don't know how.

Experience has shown that the most successful people are those who have learned to respect their own needs and the needs of others in a nurturing way.

You will create 'kids who can' by developing a thinking and caring family which knows how to enjoy everyday life as well as to cope with the unexpected.

Creating Kids Who Can *will help you to develop your child as:*

- ♦ a citizen
- ♦ a student
- ♦ a member of your family
- ♦ a friend, and
- ♦ a unique individual who enjoys the uniqueness of others

You will be delighted to realise that most of the ideas are common sense, easy to do and great fun. This book will show you how you can:

- ♦ develop your child's self esteem
- ♦ get the best out of school
- ♦ make homework an adventure
- ♦ help your child become an effective communicator
- ♦ encourage your child to be well organised

- deal with experts and have confidence in what you can do
- break down the barriers to learning maths, reading and spelling
- understand your child's behaviour
- turn your child into a learner!

Boredom will be a problem of the past. Your child will become creative, motivated, focused, purposeful and enthusiastic about developing their potential.

Our research shows that changes in education, leisure activities, family life, diet and technology can all have an effect on how children learn. Sometimes these effects are obvious, sometimes they are not.

Your child may have many complaints, such as bullying, boredom, tiredness, the work being too hard, the teacher having favourites.

The school may complain that your child is lazy, too sensitive, a bully, attention-seeking or has no concentration.

This book will show you techniques, strategies and exercises to overcome barriers to learning in both you and your child.

It will also show you how you can spot problems, work out how they have arisen and how you can find solutions which work for you and your child.

You will get to know your child better, get to understand yourself better and see your relationship with your child flourish.

Learning will stop being guesswork, happenchance and luck and become organised, structured and successful. This book will be a lifeline for learning. Do it now – you can succeed!

Jean Robb and Hilary Letts
MERSEYSIDE, AUGUST 1995

CHAPTER 1

CREATING KIDS WHO CAN

10 ATTRIBUTES FOR CONQUERING THE 21ST CENTURY!

SUCCESSFUL LEARNING TIPS

'I WANT TO HELP MY CHILD, BUT HOW?'

BARRIERS TO LEARNING

Imagine this is your child's lifeline. It started at 0 and, with the improvements in medical science (and for mathematical ease!), let's say it will continue to 100.

0_____16____25_____50_____100

This means that any period of your child's life – no matter how endless it may feel at the time – is only a fraction of that whole life span.

For example, the period before your child goes to school is only 5% of that life.

The period of 10 weeks to revise for an exam is a meagre 0.02%.

And even the whole period that your child is totally dependent on you represents but 16% of that lifeline.

Some periods will be pleasurable and others stressful, but one thing you can be sure of is that you will both need to learn new skills for each new period. These skills should give your child:

♦ real confidence
♦ competence
♦ a sense of responsibility

Confidence means being able to be flexible, to use a range of skills, to know your limits, to withstand criticism and to have realistic expectations. And when those expectations are not met, confidence means continuing with the project regardless. Confidence in children means that they are sure of their worth as people and will not see frustration of their plans as personal attacks or as evidence of their own incompetence.

Competence means a child recognises that everything is broken down into smaller parts, some of which the child will know and can use. When children feel competent they are prepared to work with others, to ask for help, to go to an expert, to attend a course or to take a back seat or the lead. Competence means recognising when events require us to reorganise the way we are working to cope with new demands.

Responsibility means a child knows how to prioritise, that the important issues in any situation have to be dealt with. Responsibility means the child finds all the available information and thinks seriously about what is helpful and what is unhelpful. Responsibility means the child will make decisions based on the information received.

Creating a confident, competent, responsible 'kid who can' will happen when you give your child support during learning. Your child might also get support from others, as long as they are able to teach in a way that leads your child to become confident, competent and responsible.

Adults give support to children when they remember children are just like us, that they are likely to be sensitive to criticism when learning something new.

You will not be giving support when you forget your child is a person. If you only worry about a child learning the facts, that child will worry when not meeting your expectations.

You won't be giving support if you worry about your own level of success – focus on how supported your child feels.

There was a time when parents felt confident about what children needed to do to stay safe, get a job or get married. Today adults do not know how to predict the world children will be living in in the future.

In this unpredictable world, we will help children best by encouraging them to become self directed so that they have a strong sense of who they are and why they are here, no matter what changes they have to deal with.

10 ATTRIBUTES FOR CONQUERING THE 21ST CENTURY

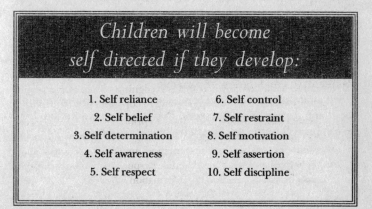

Children will become
self directed if they develop:

1. Self reliance	6. Self control
2. Self belief	7. Self restraint
3. Self determination	8. Self motivation
4. Self awareness	9. Self assertion
5. Self respect	10. Self discipline

1. Self reliance

Children who are self reliant are able to recognise their own needs and have some ideas about how they can fulfil them without hurting others: self reliant people know when to go it alone, when to accept help and when to accept not having everything their own way.

Self reliance comes from knowing how to keep yourself fed, housed, clothed, sane and solvent! It also comes from knowing how to cope with other people and new situations.

2. Self belief

If children have self belief they will have confidence that they will be all right whether the situation is stable or not: self belief is accepting one's strengths and weaknesses.

Self belief comes from coping with different situations, both expected and unexpected, and being able to build up one's own strategies for dealing with new situations.

3. Self determination

Children with self determination are able to plan, put the plan into action yet remain flexible: self determination means recognising the needs of others when planning.

Self determination comes from being given the opportunity to do an activity, with support for as long as is needed. At the same time as we offer support we should also give children encouragement to try to do more themselves.

4. Self awareness

Children with self awareness know how to stay safe in all vulnerable areas: self awareness is being well informed and confident, so avoiding fear or paranoia.

Self awareness comes from being given the opportunity to think about and discuss how we respond to different situations and how we can protect ourselves without becoming phobic.

5. Self respect

Children with self respect know who they are and where they fit in the world: self respect is believing we are equal to other people.

Self respect comes from being taught how to present oneself so that the real person is seen.

6. Self control

Self control is being able to recognise the consequences of any action: self control means knowing how to take a calculated risk.

Self control comes from learning gradually that all our actions have consequences. Children who haven't been taught about consequences are very vulnerable.

7. Self restraint

Self restraint is when we are very conscious of the needs of the situation: self restraint also means recognising our own needs.

Self restraint comes from knowing the effect of our actions and seeing alternative ways.

8. Self motivation

Self motivation is the exercise of will to help overcome all the influences that might make us avoid or stop an activity: self motivation must have some element of compromise.

Self motivation comes from experiencing the 'buzz' of achievement.

9. Self assertion

Self assertion is recognising that we are responsible for making sure others know we are human beings with thoughts and feelings as important as theirs: self assertion is not selfish, bullying or ignoring the justifiable needs of others.

Self assertion in children comes from being supported as they find their ways in the wider world. It comes from understanding how conflict arises and how it can be sorted out so that each person feels valued.

10. Self discipline

Self discipline is doing something we don't want to do but which needs to be done: self discipline can be fun and interesting.

Self discipline comes from recognising other people are not responsible for making sure we carry out our obligations.

Self doesn't have to mean selfish. By learning about themselves, children understand their impact on the world and the way the world impacts on them.

Successful Learning Tips

WHAT HAPPENS WHEN CHILDREN LEARN SOMETHING SUCCESSFULLY? THEY:

♦ KEEP AN OPEN MIND

♦ REMEMBER SOMETHING ELSE THEY LEARNED AND HOW MUCH THEY ENJOYED IT

♦ FEEL PHYSICALLY COMFORTABLE

♦ UNDERSTAND THE EXPLANATION

♦ KNOW WHAT THEY KNOW AND ARE READY TO LEARN WHAT THEY NEED TO KNOW

♦ ARE NOT FRIGHTENED OF MAKING MISTAKES

♦ ARE ABLE TO FOCUS ON THE TASK

♦ FEEL CONFIDENT THEY WILL BE ABLE TO DO IT

♦ KNOW THEY WILL NEED TO PRACTISE

♦ EXPECT THE LEARNING TO TAKE TIME

♦ ARE HAPPY TO DEVOTE TIME AND ENERGY TO THE TASK

♦ ARE NOT COMPARING THEMSELVES WITH OTHERS

♦ OBSERVE THEIR PROGRESS

♦ TAKE RESPONSIBILITY FOR CARRYING OUT WHAT IS NEEDED TO THE BEST OF THEIR ABILITIES

♦ UNDERTAKE TO STAY INVOLVED IN THE LEARNING

♦ SPEND TIME THINKING ABOUT WHAT THEY HAVE DONE – RECOGNISING WHAT WENT WELL, WHAT NEEDS TO BE IMPROVED AND WHAT DIDN'T WORK AT ALL

♦ ARE HAPPY TO ASK AND ANSWER QUESTIONS

♦ KNOW THAT FEELING DISHEARTENED IS NOT A PERMANENT OBSTACLE TO LEARNING SOMETHING NEW

'I WANT TO HELP MY CHILD, BUT HOW?'

Remember, you are your child's best friend. You have known your child all his or her life and your child wants to please you.

- ◆ You can work together.
- ◆ You can learn together.
- ◆ You can have fun together.

'I failed at school – will I be able to help my child to learn?'

Of course you will. You don't have to run a restaurant to be able to cook lovely meals for your family, you don't have to be a dress designer to sew on a button and you don't have to be a doctor to put on a Band-Aid! Just look at what you have already taught your child. Between birth and 10 she will learn to cope with everyday life, to count, read, tell the time, form letters and make sentences, to look after her belongings and stay safe. She will learn how to cooperate with other people in a variety of situations. Your child will learn best if she's confident of your love, your sense of purpose and your support.

It is only at secondary school that your child will start more specialised learning, and if you have taught her how to think and how to learn then you will have prepared her well.

'I don't have much time – how can I help?'

Decide how much time you have got and then ration it carefully. It may be that you only have time to sit and have a chat with your child about the task (e.g. setting the table or homework), but no time to help. So structure your conversation so that your child knows:

- ◆ what he is being asked to do
- ◆ how he will do it
- ◆ what equipment will be needed
- ◆ if there is anything he needs from you

If you and your child close your eyes at the end of the discussion, as in 'a going still' (see Appendix), you will help him get ready for the next part of the task. If he recognises there is protected time for the task, his attention will be focused and he will be purposeful and motivated.

'He only wants to play with his friends'

Remember, you are responsible for your child's learning! Your child needs to know that you take that responsibility seriously. And learning is a family business, so it is important you establish the need for time, effort and commitment from all the family members. Negotiating with children is important, but it is only reasonable to do it once the boundaries have been set. To learn successfully, your child needs to understand there are boundaries.

For example, if your child has homework to do but also wants to play with his friends, he can choose when he plays and when he does his homework, but he knows the homework must be done.

'How much help should I give her?'

Give sufficient help so that at the end of any activity your child will have more skill. At the end of any activity she should feel confident that she can learn well and can use her learning. If the task she has been given is too difficult, give her just a small part of it to do. By using questions, you can show her what she can do and what she already knows which will then guide her to complete the task. Never leave her feeling she is not capable of being successful.

'He seems so tired after school – more work doesn't seem fair'

There is a rhythm to everyone's day and the important thing is to discover your child's rhythm. Then decide how that rhythm can fit into the family's pace. Plan a routine which gives each person, as far as possible, an opportunity for going at their own rhythm. If your child is tired after school, discover his energy boosters – food, exercise, a cuddle, sleep, chat or read, for example. Then organise activities including homework and helping in the house to happen when he is at his best.

'*I know how to do it, but she says they do it differently at school*'

All parents at some point feel defeated by their child saying: 'we don't do it that way at school'.

Some schools have developed ways of involving parents in the children's learning. If your child's school doesn't offer help to parents or if she keeps saying you don't know how to do it, don't be put off helping her. There are several basic learning and teaching principles which are true.

CHILDREN NEED TO LEARN AND PRACTISE HOW TO:

♦ speak in a way that can be understood
♦ develop handwriting
♦ increase their spelling knowledge
♦ be polite
♦ recognise that maths is everyday life written down in symbols, and to learn how the symbols work

**YOU ARE THE PARENT:
ALWAYS TRUST YOUR OWN
COMMON SENSE.**

'Is it ever too late to help him learn?'

You can support your child whatever his age if you teach him how to learn. He will do that if he knows how to get the best out of his teachers, at home or at school.

Teachers respond well to students of whatever age who turn up on time, bring the right equipment, listen, respond to instructions, ask appropriate questions and make an effort. It also helps if students look presentable (clean clothes, clean fingernails, clean ears and nose!), look teachers in the eye, speak clearly, don't chew with their mouths open and are polite.

'His sister's clever – but he's good at sport'

Even sportsmen and women want and need to know how to read, write and spell. So, turn the three Rs into a game too, to reinforce the sporty child's strong points. Compare one of his activities or attempts against another. Note things that have improved and what he needs to practise next. And remember to list the results, check on progress and see if he can top the league in paper sports as well as field sports.

The biggest barrier we have to anything, including learning, is the way we think. The more we understand about how we think, the easier it is to discover if there's a problem – a barrier to learning – and to deal with it. We can develop strategies to improve our thinking so that lots of possibilities are available to us.

The more we understand about how what we think affects what we do, the more we have a chance of changing the effect of a barrier to learning.

Encourage your child to notice how he or she is thinking and to find out how other people are thinking.

BARRIERS TO LEARNING

Some Things to Think About!

♦ WHAT IS THINKING?

♦ WHAT DO YOU THINK ABOUT?

♦ WHAT DO YOU FIND HARD TO THINK ABOUT?

♦ DO YOU KNOW WHEN YOU DO YOUR BEST THINKING?

♦ DO YOU EVER THINK ABOUT THINKING?

♦ IS WORRYING THINKING?

♦ IS PLANNING THINKING?

♦ IS REMEMBERING THINKING?

♦ IS LEARNING THINKING?

THERE ARE NO RIGHT ANSWERS – BUT THERE'S MORE TO THINKING THAN MEETS THE EYE!

What can cause a child to have a barrier to learning?

STRESS IS HIGH ON THE LIST. STRESS CAN RESULT FROM:

- ♦ a physical condition, permanent or temporary
- ♦ a feeling of not belonging
- ♦ a feeling that I can't understand because I'm not clever enough
- ♦ past experiences
- ♦ present situation
- ♦ a feeling that I can't understand because I missed the bit that came before
- ♦ feeling like a square peg in a round hole
- ♦ a poor learning environment

What can help a child overcome a barrier to learning?

DO THE CAN-CAN

- ♦ Your child may already be someone who can!
- ♦ Your child may have barrier-free learning experiences.
- ♦ Your child can check by thinking of something he really enjoys doing.

Ask your child: 'What are you really good at?' Write down your child's answer and then make sure you cover the following ideas, in words which make sense to both of you. These questions will tell you more about how your child does something that produces a feeling of success.

- ♦ What are the skills you need to do it and how much effort will you happily put into getting better at it?
- ♦ Can you feel excited and interested by a mistake, because it gives you a chance to find out more?
- ♦ How do you get ready for the activity?
- ♦ How do you think about it before you start, while you're doing it and when you are finished?
- ♦ Do you delight in your achievement and feel happy to talk to others about it?
- ♦ Are you prepared to focus on one small part to improve?
- ♦ Are you prepared to put a lot of effort into something that appears quite small to someone else?
- ♦ How affected are you by other people's opinion of you when you are doing the activity?
- ♦ How do you make sure you give yourself the best opportunity for success?
- ♦ How do you congratulate yourself?
- ♦ Do you go at your own pace? Do you know when to take a break or to stop?
- ♦ Are you frightened or disheartened by your mistakes or by other people's greater skill?
- ♦ Do you analyse what other people have done to see what you could incorporate into your work?
- ♦ How will you rearrange your life to make sure there is time for the activity?

If your child can answer these questions then he or she is already someone who can!

And now your child can apply the same ideas to learning anything.

The learning environment

You can break down barriers to learning by creating a supportive and nurturing working environment. An environment is supportive when all the needs of the individuals working in it are recognised in a holistic way.

You can create this environment for your child by checking the following needs:

PHYSICAL
♦ tired or hungry?
♦ need to go to the toilet?
♦ need a break?

EMOTIONAL
♦ parent in right frame of mind to help?
♦ anything to tell parent or do before being able to concentrate?

INTELLECTUAL
♦ need a chat, a chance to talk about the task?

PSYCHOLOGICAL
♦ need encouragement to approach a task considered threatening, intimidating or boring?

ACADEMIC
♦ need explanation of something not known in order to do the activity? Parent may also need to explain what sort of thing the teacher is expecting, or to suggest further possibilities that the child is not aware of.

STRUCTURAL
♦ right equipment?
♦ understanding of time available for task?
♦ help with planning and checking?

♦ work best if feeling part of what's going on in house, or when working alone or with friend?

Remember, success comes from providing a supportive and nurturing working environment which works for you and your child.

Reasons for barriers to teaching your own child

Parents are often surprised to find that the barriers which arise when they try to help their own child don't exist when they teach or offer help to their child's friends. They feel helpless and hopeless with their own children. If this happens to you, don't despair – it is a very common experience.

YOU MAY FEEL:

Anxious: you feel so responsible for every part of your child's life. You don't want to threaten your child's belief that you can provide a safe haven from the hurly-burly of life. When you are helping your child's friends, you know they have their own safe havens.

Fearful that you might fail your child: you worry that you will choose the wrong time to teach, the wrong place to teach, the wrong way to teach and the wrong thing to teach. When you are helping a friend, you know that any new information you give is likely to help.

You are neglecting the rest of the family: you worry that you are giving too much attention, money, time or privileges to one child at the expense of other members of the family. When you're teaching somebody else, time is allocated to that task and the same conflicts don't arise.

Experiences you've both had in the past are getting in the way: it is sometimes hard to see what your own child can do. When you're dealing with someone else's child, you are in a better position to see potential more clearly.

Love: it is difficult to be cruel to be kind to your own child. A particular look will remind you of a time when your child was very vulnerable. This can make you doubt that you are doing the right thing. When you're dealing with someone else's child, you're prepared to go further.

Your child feels you're not able to help: your own child may turn to other people for help which you could have given. Other people's children recognise your real abilities which might help them.

Irritated: the fact that you live so close to your own child can mean your patience is already at a low ebb. For example, you know about the untidy bedroom or the experimenting with a nervous twitch. Someone else's child is unlikely to have the same effect because you have the choice of whether you help that child or not and whether to continue or stop.

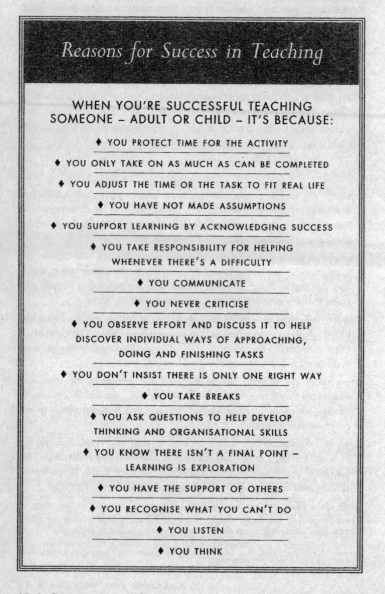

Reasons for Success in Teaching

WHEN YOU'RE SUCCESSFUL TEACHING SOMEONE – ADULT OR CHILD – IT'S BECAUSE:

♦ YOU PROTECT TIME FOR THE ACTIVITY

♦ YOU ONLY TAKE ON AS MUCH AS CAN BE COMPLETED

♦ YOU ADJUST THE TIME OR THE TASK TO FIT REAL LIFE

♦ YOU HAVE NOT MADE ASSUMPTIONS

♦ YOU SUPPORT LEARNING BY ACKNOWLEDGING SUCCESS

♦ YOU TAKE RESPONSIBILITY FOR HELPING WHENEVER THERE'S A DIFFICULTY

♦ YOU COMMUNICATE

♦ YOU NEVER CRITICISE

♦ YOU OBSERVE EFFORT AND DISCUSS IT TO HELP DISCOVER INDIVIDUAL WAYS OF APPROACHING, DOING AND FINISHING TASKS

♦ YOU DON'T INSIST THERE IS ONLY ONE RIGHT WAY

♦ YOU TAKE BREAKS

♦ YOU ASK QUESTIONS TO HELP DEVELOP THINKING AND ORGANISATIONAL SKILLS

♦ YOU KNOW THERE ISN'T A FINAL POINT – LEARNING IS EXPLORATION

♦ YOU HAVE THE SUPPORT OF OTHERS

♦ YOU RECOGNISE WHAT YOU CAN'T DO

♦ YOU LISTEN

♦ YOU THINK

If you can remember these reasons for success and use them with your child, you will be successful whenever you try to help.

Breaking through your barriers to teaching your own child

Take one reason for success in teaching others and apply it to a task you are doing with your own child.

For example, if you take on only as much as can be successfully completed, it allows you to supervise your child so that you can offer support, nurturing and instruction as appropriate. Look at the following exercise.

FIVE MINUTES TO TIDY HIS ROOM

1. Discuss with your child how he's going to do it in the time that is available.
2. Make a note of what is agreed.
3. Set a limit of a minute and see how much of the task he can get done.
4. Check how much is done.
5. Ask him if he knows what he's going to do next.
6. Check after three minutes.
7. Suggest one thing to finish in the last minute.
8. Congratulate him on his success.
9. Ask questions about how he found the job.

Discuss what needs to be done: discussion is important so that you are equals in the planning. The boundaries can be set but without creativity being stifled.

Take notes: if notes of the discussion are taken, there is a record for you both should there be a problem. By writing things down you are already approaching the task in an orderly fashion.

See how much your child can do in one minute: starting with just one minute minimises the risk of failing the whole task. Weaknesses in the design or planning of the task or the child's ability to perform the task will become clear.

Check how much has been done: when you check you will know whether the child feels good about what he or she is doing. When you feel you are getting nowhere, you want to stop.

Check what your child is going to do next: this allows your child to take charge and make his or her own decisions while still recognising that boundaries have been set. It also allows you to make suggestions if you feel they are necessary.

Check again: your experience may mean that you can give a pointer on how to rescue the job and preserve what has been done already so your child has a sense of being successful.

Congratulations! Your child will feel enthusiastic about trying again if he or she feels that something has been achieved this time. Resist the natural urge to point out how little has been done, how much is still to do and how you'd have done twice as much in half the time!

QUESTIONS HELP REFLECTION AND PLANNING FOR THE FUTURE

♦ WAS THE JOB WORTH DOING?

♦ WHAT DID YOU ENJOY MOST?

♦ WHAT DID YOU LEARN?

♦ WHAT SURPRISED YOU?

♦ IS THERE ANYTHING YOU'D DO DIFFERENTLY NEXT TIME?

Remember – learn a bit, then a bit more

Most things to do with learning are really common sense. If you're panicking, go back to what you feel you really know and then you'll have the confidence to try something new.

When you learn something new, you can be overwhelmed by all the new information. This is natural.

Remember! Go slow to go fast.

That way you'll keep on learning.

CHAPTER 2

HARNESSING PARENT POWER

HOW TO BE A PARENT AND SURVIVE THE STRAIN!

PARENT POWER AT HOME

PARENT POWER AT SCHOOL

DEALING WITH TRICKY QUESTIONS

HARNESSING GRANDPARENT POWER

HOW TO BE A PARENT
AND SURVIVE THE STRAIN!

You are human – not superhuman!

As a child you would have been determined never to make the same mistakes, be as unfair or silly as your own parents. Once you became a parent you realised this was a fantasy. The realisation that you are making the same mistakes as your parents will sometimes make you laugh and sometimes make you want to cry.

YOU WILL HARNESS YOUR POWER AS A PARENT BEST IF YOU REMEMBER THESE THINGS.

- ♦ You are human!
- ♦ Sometimes you are certain and other times very uncertain.
- ♦ Sometimes you will feel in control and sometimes out of control.
- ♦ Sometimes you will know what you are doing and sometimes you will feel completely at sea.
- ♦ Sometimes you will be able to make plans and see them through and at other times you will feel at the mercy of every unexpected visitor or request from the family.

Remember, relaxations will give you the chance to recover your balance after the emotional highs and lows brought on by parenthood. Find out more about these relaxations in the Appendix.

Remember, the emotions you experience as a parent will be like nothing you have ever experienced before. Without training and without real understanding of the responsibility you have taken on, you are suddenly aware that what you do makes a difference not just to you but also to your child. The guidance you give will determine whether your child will be able to cope with the experiences he or she meets. You will be responsible for teaching your child to become an aware adult able to take on responsibilities for self, family and community.

Remember, you had life experiences before your child came so, although your child cannot be your whole world, you will be your child's whole world while he or she is gaining independence.

Remember, your child does need to know there are things you feel certain about and things you feel uncertain about.

Remember, your child needs to know there are things which you can control, things you can modify and things you can't control at all.

Remember, you will always be doing your best for your child. As you gain more experience you may realise that you could have made a different choice. But at the time you make any decision you are always doing your best.

Remember, you find out most by asking questions, organising the information and asking questions again. What do I know? What do I need to know? How can I find out?

The A-Z of Harnessing Parent Power

Awareness	Nourishment
Belief	Organisation
Compliments	Persuasion
Decisions	Questioning
Energy	Reasoning
Friendship	Safety
Guesswork	Teaching
Humour	Understanding
Imagination	Valuing
Justice	Waiting
Keeping	Experience
Learning	Yearning
Modelling	Zeal

PARENT POWER AT HOME

WHERE IS ALL THIS PARENT POWER? WE OFTEN HEAR COMMENTS LIKE THESE FROM PARENTS WHO FEEL POWERLESS AT HOME.

♦ My child won't eat any fruit or vegetables.

♦ She watches too much TV.

- ♦ He's horrible to his sister.
- ♦ She doesn't go to sleep.
- ♦ He doesn't tidy his room.
- ♦ My mother thinks I should be more strict.
- ♦ My husband thinks taking him to karate lessons will sort him out, but I hate violence.
- ♦ I'm so busy.

PARENT POWER – AT HOME

1. Decide on one issue you want to sort out with your child. Let's say it's sensible eating.
2. Do a relaxation (see Appendix). The best one for a situation like this is 'Turning can't do into can do'.
3. Make a list of all the reasons why you're worried about your child's eating.

> IT'S NOT GOOD FOR HIS TEETH
>
> HE DOESN'T SEEM TO HAVE ENOUGH ENERGY
>
> MEAL TIMES ARE BATTLES
>
> YOU'RE FED UP WITH HEARING YOURSELF,
> AND HIM, WHINING ABOUT IT

4. Now ask your child to make his own list about what he thinks is important about his eating. Resist the temptation to add your concerns or stop him from putting down what he wants.
5. Together decide on one part of each list where you're both prepared to compromise.

> HE WILL AGREE TO EATING ONE
> PIECE OF FRUIT EVERY DAY.

6. You could have a record sheet on the fridge door.
7. When you feel that the good habit has been established, then another problem can be tackled.
8. If you also give your child a chance to tell you something that drives him up the wall about you, you can work on that at the same time - there can be two record sheets on the fridge!

Parent power at school

WHERE IS ALL THIS PARENT POWER? WE OFTEN HEAR COMMENTS LIKE THESE FROM PARENTS WHO FEEL POWERLESS AT SCHOOL.

- ♦ I am terrified when I have to speak to the teacher.
- ♦ I find waiting at the school gate very stressful.
- ♦ I find it difficult to deal with the competition between parents over their children's progress.
- ♦ I am a single parent and I think the teacher thinks all my child's problems come from that.
- ♦ We are both so busy, it's hard for us to check on her everyday progress.
- ♦ I was useless at school, so what chance has he got?

LET'S LOOK AT THESE ISSUES IN MORE DETAIL

If you feel nervous about meetings with teachers

Remember that teachers are often nervous about talking to parents. Just as parents have no training in bringing up children, teachers have no training in talking to the parents of the children they teach. Some are very good at it and will put parents at their ease. Others will deal with you as if you are the problem child.

THE BEST WAY OF COPING WITH SUCH FEELINGS IS THIS.

1 Make a list of the subjects you wish to discuss.
2 Find a time, convenient to both you and the teacher, for a meeting.
3 Make sure when you are talking with the teacher you are both on the same sized chairs.
4 Tell the teacher how nervous you are because she may think your tension is crossness.
5 Make sure that you feel physically comfortable and you're happy with the way you are presenting yourself. If having clean hair makes you feel comfortable, then wash it before you go. If the jumper you are wearing has a dirty mark, change it. You don't have to power dress, but neither do you have to dress as a victim.

If you find meeting your child at the school gate a stressful experience

You may have very strong memories of your own schooldays, but you may never have been met at the school gate. It is only in recent times that parents have felt it necessary to take their children from place to place.

If you didn't get a model of how to meet a child at the school gate you may feel unsure. When you have seen how someone else handles a particular situation, it gives you confidence – you will have an idea of what to do.

Meeting your child at the school gate can arouse memories of your own time at school as a child and you suddenly find yourself catapulted back, with the feelings you had when you were there. If your time at school was happy then you will probably approach other parents at the gate in a relaxed and friendly way. If it was unhappy, you may feel so insecure and vulnerable that meeting your child becomes a nightmare rather than a time when you can greet your child happily and renew your bond.

Meeting at the school gate should be a positive time and a chance to share the worlds you have been in while apart.

If you hate the competition between parents over their children's progress

The first rule for creating a successful child is never to compare. The chances of you never breaking this rule are slim!

However, avoid those situations where other parents make you feel intimidated. When you do find yourself comparing your child with a cousin, classmate or the child next door, remember that self restraint is a very important quality to develop - not just for your child but also for you!

If you observe your child's progress and observe the progress of others, you will find information which will help you to help your child.

Whenever you are worried, it is important not to make yourself more vulnerable. If you talk to someone about your worries and they don't help you feel more able to cope, don't see that as your weakness, just look for help somewhere else.

If you feel vulnerable as a single parent

First of all, the school may not think that your child's problems are related to you being a single parent. Most children will have problems at some point in their school career. The quality of the parenting that your child gets has nothing to do with whether he or she lives with a single parent or not.

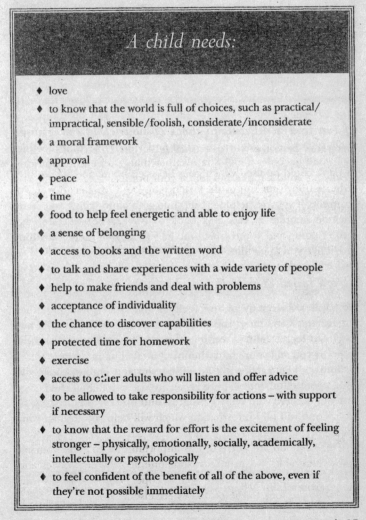

A child needs:

♦ love
♦ to know that the world is full of choices, such as practical/impractical, sensible/foolish, considerate/inconsiderate
♦ a moral framework
♦ approval
♦ peace
♦ time
♦ food to help feel energetic and able to enjoy life
♦ a sense of belonging
♦ access to books and the written word
♦ to talk and share experiences with a wide variety of people
♦ help to make friends and deal with problems
♦ acceptance of individuality
♦ the chance to discover capabilities
♦ protected time for homework
♦ exercise
♦ access to other adults who will listen and offer advice
♦ to be allowed to take responsibility for actions – with support if necessary
♦ to know that the reward for effort is the excitement of feeling stronger – physically, emotionally, socially, academically, intellectually or psychologically
♦ to feel confident of the benefit of all of the above, even if they're not possible immediately

If you find it difficult to check on your child's everyday progress because you are unable to get to school

A book could be used which goes between home and school with information from you to the teacher and the teacher to you. For example, if you are helping your child with handwriting you could include samples of this in a book so the teacher can see what you're doing and at the same time let you know if there's anything she'd like you to include.

If you failed at school

You will know many of the feelings that your child has when attempting something. You will be frightened that your child may begin to feel a failure. You may need to have someone who can support you and your child when you are feeling insecure.

Your child's teacher will be seeing you as a parent, concerned about your child. She will not be seeing you as a failing child.

DEALING WITH TRICKY QUESTIONS

Tricky questions really revolve around the issues of freedom, safety and responsibility where you have to make decisions. In some cases there is a law which supports your decision. For example, your child has to go to school and has to wear a seat belt. But many times the decision is left up to you. Use your common sense and trust that you know what is best.

How can I let my child do what she wants and still feel in control?

AN EXERCISE FOR PLANNING YOUR TIME SO YOU STAY IN CONTROL

Think about the following questions:

1. What sort of life do you want for your family?
2. How much time do you want to spend together as a family?
3. How much time do you want to spend individually with each child? This time might be used for:

HELPING WITH HOMEWORK

DOING HOUSEHOLD CHORES TOGETHER

PLAYING GAMES, TALKING, EATING, WATCHING TV

4. How much time are you happy for your child to spend following his or her own interests?
5. What time do you feel your child should go to bed/stay up?

AN EXERCISE FOR PLANNING YOUR CHILD'S TIME

1. Write down the number of hours where your child has freedom of choice.
2. Write down all the things your child wants to do.
3. Decide how much time your child wants to allocate to each activity.
4. Now you can discuss together what makes sense.

By thinking of these questions and doing the exercises, you will show your child how to plan and take into consideration other's needs, safety factors, time limits, geographical limits, financial limits and responsibilities.

Remember, every family is unique. At any time, even within a family which feels that everything is working efficiently, something may change – the cat will need taking to the vet. This will disturb all your best laid plans, particularly if every last minute is planned for. Try to leave some slack in your timetabling where options can be taken up and emergencies can be dealt with.

How can I make sure my child does his homework?

AN EXERCISE FOR PLANNING HOMEWORK TOGETHER

1. Sit down as friends who are going to work together.
2. Check the homework diary.
3. Both of you write for a minute on what needs to be done.
4. Decide on the time available.
5. Talk about what the teacher will be expecting.
6. Decide on any equipment or other material needed and any help needed.

7. Make a timetable, including dates by which the work should be finished.
8. Collect equipment.
9. Arrange the time when you will check on how the work is going.
10. Check whether your child can get on with it now.
11. Review the session and talk about what you have both learned and noticed.

How can I make sure she uses some of the things she's given? She has so many toys that just sit in the cupboard. How can I get her to play with them?

AN EXERCISE FOR GETTING
THE MOST OUT OF A GAME, TOY OR ACTIVITY

1. Take the game out of the cupboard.

2. The first question to ask is: 'What can you see?'

3. Write down your answers as well as hers. Possible answers are a box, some writing (on the lid), a game, don't know, a picture (on the lid).

4. The next question is: 'What do you think you can do with it?' This is an important question because she is being given the chance to be creative. Resist the temptation to make comments about the ideas, simply record them on paper.

5. Then ask what could be done next. Your child may want to take off the lid, put the toy away or tip everything out. If she wants to put the toy away you may decide to agree but plan another time when you'll come back to it. You may realise that the toy is too difficult and put it away for some time in the future. You may decide to persist and arouse your child's interest in the next stage.

6. If your child wants to take off the lid, let that happen and allow her to explore the game as far as she is able, supporting her when her interest or competence flags. You can give support by asking questions rather than taking control.

7. Sometimes the toy could need more skill than your child has and you could help so that she can continue the game.

8. When your child is showing no interest in a toy or is using it inappropriately, you can motivate her by finding out as much as you can about what she already knows and then telling her the next bit.

9. Sometimes she will want to learn to sew, knit or ride a bike and you feel confident that she will ask for help when it is needed, or you will recognise where help is required, because she has such an interest in learning the skill.

How can I make sure he is safe? He wants to walk to school by himself but I'm too scared to let him. What do I do about freedom to go unaccompanied by an adult?

There are no hard and fast rules because you have to assess the likelihood of danger in your own area. The decision you make will always be a trade-off between your desire to let your child explore his world for himself and your desire to keep him safe.

You can't protect your child from a drunk driver, a natural disaster or a freak accident. In all of these cases, it's a matter of being in the wrong place at the wrong time and in no way could it have been predicted or guarded against.

If your child knows your rules for roaming, he should be able to explore whilst maximising his opportunities for independence and minimising the risk. These rules should include your child:

- knowing his phone number and address and your work number
- knowing that a designated person must be kept informed of where he is at all times
- knowing that arrangements must not be changed without notice
- knowing your child must always arrange a meeting point when you are out, in case he is separated from you
- repeating to you what arrangements have been made so that you can check he is still clear on the details
- making sure he only goes out if he has the right equipment - hat for the sun, helmet for riding a bike, money for the phone and so on
- checking with an adult that it is all right to go
- saying what time he is leaving and coming back
- saying where he is going and who is going with him
- checking that the outing is safe and fits in with the needs of others

Your child needs to know that whenever he is on his own it gives you a chance to see how much independence you can give him next time.

Your child can still go out if an outing doesn't work, but you will need to discuss what went wrong and what alternative things he could do to make it work next time.

Your child needs to know that he must not get into a car with a drunk driver, go with a stranger or stay at an event that is difficult, but will have to go to a place which is safe or ring you.

Children need to know which places are safe in case they are ever stuck. You can discuss places you are happy for him to go, such as the police station, a friend's house or the library.

How can I be sure it's all right for your child to be obsessed?

Your child could be obsessed by television, computers, friends, books, an idol, religion or a hobby.

Obsessions are a part of growing up and if they are contributing to the all-round development of your child then they may be beneficial. If it's helping her learning, she's meeting new people, taking on responsibilities and you are seeing new capabilities, it can all be part of her becoming a member of the wider society.

Often what you're offering isn't what she wants at the time – what she wants can't be offered by you. This doesn't mean she doesn't love you.

On the other hand, does the obsession interfere with her sleep, schoolwork or family life, change her behaviour or lead her to steal or tell lies?

If your child is obsessed and it is an unhealthy obsession like this, you can help by suggesting ways of restoring a balance. For example, you might discuss what time can be spent on the activity and explain how important it is that she take on her share of responsibility for herself.

Make sure an obsession doesn't interfere with your family life. Trust your own common sense and establish a time when all the people in the house come together for a drink or a chat before going to bed.

Should I be worried about computers?

- ◆ Does he seem to spend a lot of time playing on them?
- ◆ Does he get very irritable when he's playing?
- ◆ Has he stopped talking to you?
- ◆ Do you know what programs he is using?
- ◆ Does he still read?
- ◆ Is he still playing sport?

Some children do become computer addicts and find it hard to drag themselves away from the screens. If it's interfering with family life or school work, then try to explain to your child why it's important to do other things.

Don't let technology control you. It can be hard for you to know how to deal with something you didn't have as a child, because it's difficult to know where the risks or benefits are. Part of your conversations with your child can involve computers. What does your child think you need to know about them? Ask your child to be your teacher. Find a time to explore and learn together.

How can I make sure she goes out and meets other people? How can I help her feel good about herself?

YOUR CHILD THINKS SHE LOOKS HORRIBLE BECAUSE SHE IS:

♦ too fat
♦ too thin
♦ the smallest in the class
♦ short-sighted and wears glasses

You need to give your child the experience that will help her really understand that all people are different.

AN EXERCISE IN SELF ESTEEM

1. Talk with your child about how she would like to look. Make the description as detailed as possible.
2. Draw up a chart together.
3. Find a place where a lot of children can be seen.
4. Note down the characteristics of say every tenth child.
5. Decide where these would fit on the chart.
6. Count how many children you have seen that fit your child's model of an ideal person.

This will help her to realise that very few people are perfectly packaged!

Sometimes it can help to ask family members or friends what they would like to change about themselves. When she realises that lots of people she think look all right would actually prefer to look different, she will be able to move on and start to think of ways to create her own style.

How to cope with bullying

If your child is being bullied you will want to sort out the problem. Talk to your child about what is happening, where it is happening and who is doing the bullying.

Ask what your child would like you to do to help. Your child may want to sort out the problem alone, but be confident of your support.

If the bullying is happening at school and your child asks you to help, contact the school and arrange a meeting to talk to a member of staff. Ask for a copy of the rules the school uses to cope with bullying.

Prepare some notes with your child before the meeting so you are clear about the details. If it helps you feel better, ask a friend to go to the meeting with you.

TAKE NOTES AT THE MEETING AND MAKE SURE YOU ARE CLEAR ABOUT:

- ♦ what the school is going to do
- ♦ what the school expects you to do
- ♦ what the school would like your child to do

If the bullying happens outside school, try to follow a similar plan. Because bullying is a relationship problem, the best solution is one that has been sorted out and agreed with both parties. Both parties should feel valued, respect each others needs and feelings and understand why a solution needs to be found.

If you do arrange a meeting with other parents and children, keep a record of the discussion and make sure everyone involved is clear that what they have said has been heard in the way they wanted.

Harnessing grandparent power

If you already have a happy relationship with your child's grandparents you will know some of the benefits grandparents can give, not just to your child but also to you.

However, lots of parents feel under pressure from grandparents. Grandparents can feel, to the new parents, like cuckoos edging them out of the nest while cooing over the baby.

But if you can find a way to negotiate how your child's grandparents can take part in his or her life, it will be of benefit to everyone involved.

Grandparents can:

♦ go at a pace which is closer to your child's pace

♦ offer protected time for grandchildren because it is often on a prearranged basis, grandparents can allocate their time knowing it has a beginning and an end

♦ see traits which your child shares with other members of the extended family – grandparents do not see your child as a sum total, but as having similarities to many family members

♦ rearrange their schedules to help your child

♦ reassure you about your child

♦ use their experience to benefit your child

Being a grandparent of kids who can

You get no training in how to be grandparents. You may dream about what you will do when your grandchild arrives. You may have decided that your grandchild's arrival will have little impact on your life. But the reality is usually very different, even for grandparents who live a long way away or are working. The birth of a new child is a time of heightened emotions for all concerned and you can't predict how you will feel or what changes your grandchild will make to your lifestyle. Becoming a grandparent is often a time of great change.

You may feel responsible and hope that you have given your own child all the skills necessary to cope with this precious new bundle.

You may remember how much you resented older people

telling you what to do when you felt vulnerable and inexperienced as a new parent. You may have vowed not to do the same thing to your own children as they become parents.

But you have lived longer. You have brought children through to adulthood successfully. You do know what measles spots look like. All your good resolutions about leaving your adult children to make their own mistakes can simply disappear when a new baby arrives and you become a grandparent.

The arrival of the first grandchild marks the beginning of a new generation. There is a sense of magic as the baby represents the family projecting far into the future. The baby's birth means that family life will never be the same because of all the new possibilities that having a baby in the family brings.

Just as you learned to be a parent by talking to others and sharing the highs and lows, now you may need to talk to other grandparents. You will be amazed to find how many people share the same worries and delights as you do!

WHY CHILDREN STUMBLE

DID THEY FALL...

...OR WERE THEY PUSHED?

KIDS WITH NO CONFIDENCE

KIDS WITH MISPLACED CONFIDENCE

THE LEARNING ENVIRONMENT

ONE STEP AT A TIME

EDUCATION MATTERS

The A-Z of falling down

CHILDREN WHO STUMBLE:

Always talk in class
Believe they've got it right
Clown around
Don't listen
Expect to be told at least twice
Fiddle about
Guess wildly
Have no idea what they're supposed to do
Irritate teachers because they think it's funny
Jump in without thinking
Keep getting up and walking around
Lose their pencils
Make silly mistakes
Never look where they're supposed to be looking
Only work when someone sits next to them
Pretend they're working
Quarrelsome – always causing a disturbance
Read carelessly
Stare into space
Tell tales
Untidy
Visible – always the ones the teacher notices
Write badly – their books look a mess
eXasperating
Yawn – and make you feel tired too
laZy – and appear not to care

Your child may stumble for many reasons. Children who don't understand what is expected will *fall down* in a classroom situation because they won't know what to look at, when to look at it or even how they're supposed to look. Learning is about knowing when to pay attention.

If you recognise your child in this A-Z, or if teachers have mentioned that your child could be doing better, then the suggestions below will help turn your child into a kid who can!

Let's take a look at examples of each of the stumbling blocks we've listed.

Always talking

Fiona couldn't understand why nobody liked her. In class she would try to chat to the other children when they wanted to get on with their work. Explain to a child like Fiona that there is a time for working and a time for talking.

Believes he's got it right

Ian thought whatever he wrote down as the answer had to be right because he'd written it down. A child like Ian can be helped by watching everything he does and gently letting him know the moment he begins to get it wrong.

Clowns around

Mark loved to clown around. He thought he went to school to entertain everybody else. Mark needed to know other people had rights – the right to be quiet, the right to get on with work. Mark began to work and have fun too!

Doesn't listen

Sally was so busy chattering she didn't actually hear anything anyone said. She exhausted everyone around her. Once she learned to relax, she realised she could learn from other people. Once she was quieter, other people wanted to teach her.

Expects to be told at least twice

Colin wasted time waiting for a personal invitation to do anything. If your child wastes time, explain it's your time he's wasting. Since you haven't got time to waste, you won't be able to help him with something he needed you to do, or he has to help you with something you have to do in order to make up the time.

Fiddles about

Jody fiddles about with pens or other belongings and disturbs the teacher as well as others in the class. She does not realise how annoying it is, and feels picked on if she gets told off. She needs to know it is her behaviour that is unfair – she's ruining other children's chances to concentrate and learn.

Guesses wildly

Diane thinks that any answer is what the teacher wants. The best way to deal with this is to tell her she has to think for one minute before giving an answer.

He has no idea what he's supposed to do

Peter always shrugs and says 'I have no idea at all about what I am supposed to be doing', which makes the teacher, or whoever is helping him, feel insulted. He needs to know how to get started and then get help, so that instead he might start saying: 'I can get started, but I'm worried I will get stuck. Could you help me if I do?'.

Irritates the teacher because he thinks it is funny

Tom doesn't know when to stop. It's a case of something starting off as funny and ending up as painful. He needs help to put the brakes on. He needs to know how and when to stop himself.

Jumps in without thinking

Josephine is so busy seeing the thing that is coming next that she never really notices what's in front of her. If your child is like this, ask her first what she is doing and then what she is supposed to be doing. Gradually she will realise there should be an order to her work, and that what is happening now matters more than what is going to happen next.

Keeps getting up and walking around

This is a way of avoiding something but it can end up as a habit. Give him a task to do that you know he can manage. Insist he does it without wandering around so you begin to break the habit.

Loses her pencil

No child should have only one pencil. If your child loses her pencils, you can help by supplying her with several and getting her to run through a checklist of what she needs before she starts each morning, so she takes them with her.

Makes silly mistakes

Get him to realise there are lots of bits of any piece of work which he can do. One way of doing this is to take a thick, serious-looking book and show him how many words on a page he can actually read. It's the same for any piece of work – there will be lots of bits he can do without making mistakes.

Never looks where she's supposed to be looking

Amanda hasn't realised she's involved. She's not sure why she is there. Get her to do an observation exercise so she gradually realises how much information is available to her if she only looks.

Only works when someone sits next to him

Ask him to do as much as he can in one minute. Sit next to him for the first minute but gradually move further away. Keep a close check and, if he stops working, get him to explain why and sit by him again until he's got started. Keep repeating the procedure until he can work on his own.

Pretends she's working

Kelly is brilliant at looking like she is working. She looks studious and well prepared. Such children can be difficult to spot until it is too late. They need to know that the only person who suffers when they don't do anything is themselves, so when they are ready to work they will get going.

Quarrelsome

Luke will come and tell you the minute anyone does anything he thinks you should know about! He needs to know how hurtful this can be for others. He needs to know the teacher values Luke telling her about important things, but that some things are not important and he must try to work out the difference.

Reads carelessly

Sandy has mastered the art of reading but continues to read carelessly. It could be that she doesn't understand that she should be getting better and better, she doesn't realise that by reading properly she will get information, or she doesn't know how to read to get the meaning.

Stares into space

Staring into space can make a teacher think Patrick is not listening when he is. He needs to know that the teacher will think he's listening if he looks at her and will think he's working if he looks at his book.

Tells tales

Linda appears to tell lies but is really telling tales. She wants the real world to be the way she says it is. She's not really out to trick anybody, she just wants the world to be different. A child like this needs to know that after she's told a 'tale', she should let someone know that it was a 'wannabe' story and not true!

Untidy

Making an effort to be tidy can mean a child is halfway to getting good teaching. Sloppy work looks like a child doesn't care.

Visible

A child can be visible because she has a deep voice or distinctive hair or is wearing something different. She needs to know that anything she does will be spotted more quickly. She may have to live with the problem, but there may also be ways she could reduce her visibility.

If it's the way the child behaves that keeps attracting the teacher's attention, ask her how she thinks she could change her behaviour so the teacher's attention can be used for teaching. Remind her that she goes to school to work.

Writes badly

There will be times in a child's life when teachers have to write reports, and the child's books will be one of the things the teacher remembers. Teachers are human and will enjoy marking a page which is well set out and readable. Sometimes children write so badly that it's difficult to know what has been written and whether the spelling is right or wrong.

Exasperating

John has had all the explanations, all the support and all the understanding and *still* he hasn't changed. He is in danger of losing everyone's sympathy because he doesn't seem to be giving anything back. John needs to know that he does need other people's support and he must try to find ways both to help them to help him and to help himself.

Yawns

Emma yawns because she feels so overwhelmed, so tired, and she hopes the yawning will stop the teaching. If your child does this, you will know how tired you can feel. To help her break this habit, find some bit of the work that she can do and get her to practise that. When she feels more confident she can move on. She needs to know that she will eventually be able to do the whole task, but she has to give herself the chance to practise the little bits.

Lazy and appears not to care

Mary uses every technique she can think of to avoid work. She turns up late, gets ready to go early, takes ages to open her book and then finds she needs a ruler. She knows how to meander through the day and avoids or ignores pressure. By praising a child like this for what she has done you can get her to recognise the pleasurable possibilities if she *does* work.

... OR WERE THEY PUSHED?

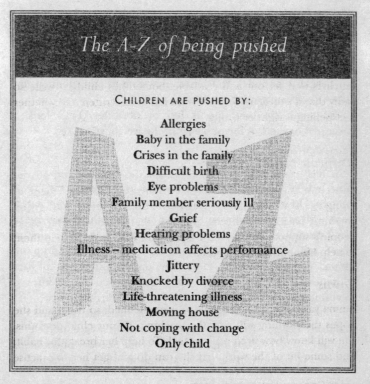

The A-Z of being pushed

CHILDREN ARE PUSHED BY:

Allergies
Baby in the family
Crises in the family
Difficult birth
Eye problems
Family member seriously ill
Grief
Hearing problems
Illness – medication affects performance
Jittery
Knocked by divorce
Life-threatening illness
Moving house
Not coping with change
Only child

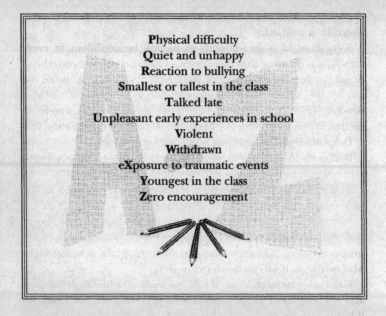

Physical difficulty
Quiet and unhappy
Reaction to bullying
Smallest or tallest in the class
Talked late
Unpleasant early experiences in school
Violent
Withdrawn
eXposure to traumatic events
Youngest in the class
Zero encouragement

Your child may be stumbling from being *pushed* by events in life – physical or emotional. Your child may *want* to pay attention, but other things are getting in the way.

For some children, life is full of obstacles. Let's look at examples of some of the obstacles in the list above.

Difficult birth

Tony was premature and spent the first two years of his life on oxygen. He was, and is, very fragile. The restrictions Tony had to cope with as a small baby and toddler meant that he missed out on the experiences that children normally have by the time they are three and a half. These include being hugged, bounced up and down, cuddled and all the other opportunities for physical closeness that babies enjoy. Tony also missed the chance of realising what a delight he could be to an adoring audience.

Tony is an example of the problems that can be caused by medical success. Tony was kept alive and it was a miracle he survived. But for Tony that means now he needs a phenomenal amount of support. If he gets that support when it is needed he changes dramatically, but just when that support is needed can't always be predicted.

Sometimes in a session with us he will be confident in every activity, just knowing that there is somebody there if he needs them. At other times he will need an adult sitting with him available the minute he needs them to support him. The physical distance between Tony and the adult when he is confident can be two to six metres. When his confidence has gone, it is 0 to 50 centimetres.

Despite his problems, Tony is making rapid progress.

If experts looked just at what Tony can do now compared with other children of the same age, they would be concerned.

But if they had seen how fast Tony's progress has been in the last two months, they would be delighted.

When you take your child to an expert, for any reason, he or she will be checking whether your child can do something properly or not. Children who can do it will get a tick, but those who nearly do it will probably get nothing.

Use your common sense. If you can see your child is developing and learning more skills, you know he is getting on. For example, if last month he couldn't tie his shoe laces and this month he can, he is making progress.

Exposure to trauma

If your child has suffered a trauma of some kind, it is important that the people working with him are sympathetic. Being sympathetic means recognising your child will need help to catch up with other children the same age. Such children:

- ♦ may need more rest than other children who have not been ill
- ♦ may need things explained if they have missed them
- ♦ may need to be reminded that they are at school to do their best
- ♦ may need support when they feel vulnerable because of what has happened
- ♦ must give reasons, not excuses, if they don't do their work
- ♦ may need help to re-establish old friendships and/or make new ones

Above all, such children must be given the chance to reach their potential.

Life-threatening illness

At eighteen months James had leukaemia and was ill for several years. He was traumatised and needed time to adjust to not being the centre of the world, school, his family and his brothers. He was frightened of being ill again. School was difficult because he had missed so much. He was lonely and fearful, but his teachers saw his low achievement as evidence that he wasn't very bright.

Remember, your child cannot always have everything he wants, when he wants it. He needs to know other people have problems, sensitivities and priorities. He needs to realise he lives in a community – home, the classroom, school – and that other people have to come first at least sometimes.

Physical difficulty

Kevin suffered muscular dystrophy and at six years old was labelled by teachers as lazy or incapable because he could not copy from the board. But the board was behind him in the classroom and the effort involved for Kevin to turn around to see it was beyond him. The school believed that if Kevin was capable or wanted to copy, then he would turn around.

Allergies

If you can't work out why your child has problems, it could be a question of allergies.

CHILDREN WITH ALLERGIES MAY SOMETIMES BE:

RELAXED, CHEERFUL, LOVING, FUN TO BE WITH, BRIGHT,
ENERGETIC, ABLE TO PAY ATTENTION AND SETTLE DOWN
TO SOMETHING THEY WANT TO DO.

BUT THEN AT OTHER TIMES THEY ARE:

MOODY, WHINGEING, OUT OF CONTROL, ANGRY, DEFIANT, WEEPY,
CLUMSY, DEPRESSED, UNHEALTHY-LOOKING WITH DARK CIRCLES UNDER
THEIR EYES, ITCHY, SILLY AND OVERLY TALKATIVE, HOSTILE, SLEEPY
(SOMETIMES SO SLEEPY THEY JUST FALL INTO BED EXHAUSTED),
UNABLE TO LEARN, NOT INTERESTED IN ANYTHING.

A CHILD WITH ALLERGIES MAY ALSO:

DROOL, HAVE ACHING MUSCLES, COMPLAIN
OF HEADACHES AND PAINS IN THE JOINTS.

Although this could be a description of any child, when it is an allergy causing the behaviour it will be impossible to jolly the child out of it.

Such a child will be as unhappy about what is happening as you are, but will probably only show it by being lethargic or grumpy.

FROM HYPERACTIVE
TO HARD WORKING

Amy was five and her school wanted to expel her. She was noisy, clumsy and hyperactive. She was also very defiant.

Her mum thought that Amy might be allergic to something so had stopped her drinking orange juice but that didn't seem to have any effect.

After Amy had been really naughty again her mum thought about what else she had eaten. She worked out that it was rusks that were upsetting Amy.

When Amy stopped eating the rusks her horrible behaviour stopped and the real Amy came through. She became relaxed, hard working, and a joy to be with.

If you think your child suffers from allergies, keep a record of your child's behaviour and what has been eaten. Does some behaviour only happen after your child has eaten a particular food? It could be that your child is allergic to that food.

If food doesn't seem to cause the problem, think what else your child may have come into contact with. Soap, polishes and other items can all cause allergic reactions. A book on allergies will give you ideas for diets and therapies that will help.

Advice versus intuition

With many of these 'stumbling blocks', you may want to seek some expert advice, but be aware that experts can so easily fit your child into a mould.

IT IS IMPORTANT THAT CHILDREN ARE NOT LIMITED BY WHAT OTHER PEOPLE THINK THEY CAN DO.

Talk to someone you know and trust, or someone who you don't know but who will listen. As a parent you are vulnerable, but remember you are the steward of your child. Beware of people who say 'I never had that problem' or 'just go and see a specialist'. These are dismissive answers. Not all advice is helpful, and some can be damaging.

Make a note! When things get difficult it can be hard to think straight, so make a list. Better still, make two. In one, list all the good things – the child's achievements, talents and successes. In the second, jot down all the negatives – the child's failures, worries and problems. Make sure your lists relate to the child not the parent.

It is vital to listen to your child and to take action to solve problems when the child cannot solve them alone.

Sometimes children may not learn because they feel so insecure and give the impression they can't learn. They also make it impossible for anyone to teach them. If you have a child like this, you have to show that you are going to help because you love them. You can teach your child how to look people in the eye, ask questions sensibly, speak when spoken to and act like other people of the same age. You can teach your child confidence.

KIDS WITH NO CONFIDENCE

TALLEST, YOUNGEST, LEAST CONFIDENT

At 14 Joe refused to go to school any more. He had walked out of school during a maths lesson saying that school was a waste of time. His mother was distraught.

When Joe talked about his schoolwork it was obvious he believed he was stupid. He was in the lowest stream and everyone, including him, messed about in lessons. Joe had realised that he was getting too close to having to find a job to keep behaving like that, but he couldn't see any way out.

Joe had not been taught algebra because it was considered too hard for the class he was in. He was seen as slow-witted and having no concentration.

At his first session, we went through some algebra and within ten minutes he had mastered the basic principles. This showed us, and him, that he was certainly not slow-witted.

The next night he came for a two hour session and concentrated throughout, learning even more complicated algebra.

Joe:

- ◆ was a classic case of a child with no confidence
- ◆ was the tallest child in the class
- ◆ was also the youngest in the class
- ◆ had teachers who – when he started school – had expected him to behave as if he was the oldest child in the class because he was tall, but forgot that he was actually the youngest
- ◆ had a slow, hesitant but thoughtful way of speaking. In school, because of time limitations, the slow and hesitant part of his speech were noticed rather than the thoughtful parts.
- ◆ had poor experience of adults trying to help him with his learning
- ◆ believed he was stupid
- ◆ had teachers who believed he couldn't be taught
- ◆ behaved like a hooligan because of his anger at the way he was being treated

Joe is one example of a child with no confidence because of events outside his control, in Joe's case his birthdate and his size.

What we did for Joe

To uncover the effect on Joe of his experiences at school, we gave him a series of maths questions and he demonstrated that he could learn quickly. He also knew how to ask questions when he wasn't sure of what to do. We were then able to show him that he was capable of being taught rapidly enough for him to improve so that the school would allow him to move up maths classes.

His confidence improved sufficiently for him to ask for English classes.

Joe's spelling and essay writing were poor but, as with maths, once he understood the skills he could use them effectively.

We discussed with him the effect that his height and his age had on teachers. We went on to explain how he had been caught in a vicious circle where his height and age meant teachers thought he couldn't be taught. Because he thought he couldn't be taught, he was not able to present himself to his teachers as someone they could help.

Children like Joe who are misunderstood simply because of the way they look are common. Other such children include:

SMALL CHILDREN

FAT CHILDREN

CHILDREN WITH A SQUINT

CHILDREN WHO NEED STRONG GLASSES

CHILDREN WHO LOOK CONFUSED BECAUSE THEY
ARE DEAF OR CAN'T HEAR PROPERLY

CHILDREN WHO ARE ON MEDICATION WHICH HAS AFFECTED
THEM PHYSICALLY, FOR EXAMPLE THEY DRIBBLE, THEY ARE
SLOW OR THEY HAVE A PHYSICAL APPEARANCE WHICH IS
DIFFERENT FROM MOST PEOPLE. WHEN THEY COME OFF
THE MEDICATION THERE IS ALSO A DANGER THAT PEOPLE
WILL STILL TREAT THEM THE WAY THEY DID BEFORE.

If you are concerned about your child being misunderstood because of physical appearance, check whether your child's potential has been recognised, for example by noticing whether your child says things which demonstrate better thinking than other people would have presumed.

IF CHILDREN'S POTENTIAL IS NOT RECOGNISED, THERE IS A DANGER THAT THEIR ABILITY TO BE TAUGHT WILL BE OVERLOOKED.

In a classroom this can mean that although a child has the same problem with the work as another child, the other child may get help because the teacher feels it is a better use of time. A child who doesn't get help will gradually stop asking for it, and end up not knowing how to do the work the rest of the class is doing. When that child falls behind that will be taken as proof of the fact that the child couldn't manage the work anyway. The child will begin to believe that too.

KIDS WITH MISPLACED CONFIDENCE

Some children stumble because they have no confidence, while others stumble because they are very confident but that confidence is misplaced.

MISPLACED CONFIDENCE

Mark was six years old when we first saw him. His main problems were that he was disruptive at school and he was poor at maths. His relationship with his teacher at school was good and she was as confused about his inability to learn as his parents. His parents were worried that he might be dyslexic or hyper active, but when we gave him the first learning task it was obvious that Mark could concentrate and enjoyed thinking. His problems became apparent when he moved on to another task and didn't get it right. He began to wriggle and would only cast fleeting glances at what he was being asked to do.

Mark:

♦ Mark had confidence because he was memorising everything he thought he needed to know

♦ had confidence he would be successful, and became totally confused when he wasn't

♦ could grasp the beginning and end of a problem or task, but missed the middle

- could not stop wriggling when he was unsuccessful, which made it difficult to teach him
- became anxious because he put unrealistic demands on himself
- felt it was his responsibility to sort a problem out once he failed
- couldn't recognise the help teachers could give

In a school situation, all of these contributed to Mark being disruptive and failing to learn. He was trying to take responsibility for his own learning too early, and becoming confused by failure. When he had nothing productive to do, he messed about.

What we did for Mark

To make sure Mark memorised everything he needed to know, we began teaching him to take in the whole of the problem, rather than jumping to conclusions.

He was encouraged to tell us what he could see, what he thought he was supposed to do and what he was going to do. Then we could see which bits of the problem he was not noticing.

We taught Mark how to relax so that he could take the pressure off himself and get the best out of anyone helping him, including his teacher.

The result was that within a week Mark was succeeding at school and able to accept help at home. He had become confident, competent and responsible.

If you think your child could be like Mark, see if you can work out the reasons for the confidence. Confidence can range from a real understanding of the situation to just thinking you can do it. Don't assume that if a child is confident in one situation the same child will be confident in every situation. If your child can't do something but seems confident, decide if any of the confidence is misplaced.

What makes kids feel confident?

CONFIDENCE IN CHILDREN CAN COME FROM A NUMBER OF SOURCES.

♦ **A real understanding of what they are doing:** their confidence is justified — they know what needs to be done and how to do it.

♦ **A belief that they have done something similar before and it's worked:** this may be true, but children might not realise the subtle differences between the new situation and the old.

♦ **A belief that a sibling can stand up for them:** this can cause problems if children have not realised that they will be held responsible for their behaviour, and that their siblings only have to help in a crisis.

♦ **Thinking they can because they don't really know what is being asked:** such children are often unsuccessful because if they don't really know what is required, they won't be able to do it.

♦ **Thinking they can because they don't know the dangers:** sometimes this can make a 'have a go' kid rather than an 'I can't' kid. There is always a risk, but some parents feel that it is a risk worth taking in order for the child to become more independent.

♦ **Thinking they can because an idol does it:** in this case you can just hope that your child has chosen a good idol! Remind your child that the idol is human and may do something your child doesn't like or shouldn't follow, and that it is your child's responsibility not to follow the idol blindly.

♦ **Thinking they can because nobody has ever stopped them, so they don't know what is likely to happen:** this can be good, but such children will need your support if things go wrong.

♦ **Thinking they know what is expected:** they may only half understand what is needed, but will try to do it.

- ◆ **A feeling you will support them:** support for adventuring physically, intellectually or socially will help a child to grow. Children know they have your support when they have been given the skills they need to try an activity.

- ◆ **Thinking that is what's wanted:** this happens when children are trying to be independent but haven't really understood how to check what is needed.

- ◆ **Thinking that what they do will help:** this is the child who decides that because you're too busy she will make the tea, without ever having done it before.

- ◆ **Doing it on behalf of someone else:** as long as it's someone else's problem, these children are lions, but when it comes to their own problems they are mice!

Misplaced confidence can be disabling because children do not understand why they have failed or why they have failed in a particular situation. Disappointment because of misplaced confidence can set up barriers to learning which take a long time to break down.

Misplaced confidence might *not* set up a barrier. It *can* be the springboard for further learning if the child is intrigued or challenged to find out more about why something isn't working and goes on to gain real confidence.

Real confidence is enabling because it allows a child to adjust to whatever situation comes along. You only change misplaced confidence into real confidence by creating a dialogue.

Remember, a dialogue is not a monologue with you saying 'Do you understand?' and your child saying 'Yes'! A dialogue happens when your child asks you a question to gain your help to understand, or to find out more, so that next time he or she might be able to go further alone.

Richard was 16 and about to do an important exam. We knew his chances of passing were slight but he had confidence that he had worked out how to be successful himself. In his mind, success meant getting teachers or parents off his back. Adults had tried to persuade him that what he was doing would not help, but he had not understood why they were concerned. He had not realised that his old ways of measuring success had become redundant. He wanted to become a fireman and to do that he needed qualifications. Ten weeks before his exams he suddenly recognised that his confidence in knowing how to operate was misplaced. He began to ask for help, and the dialogue began.

THE LEARNING ENVIRONMENT

THE BOY WHO LEARNT
WHEN HIS DAD DIDI

Ken, aged seven, couldn't read. Every night his dad worked on his reading with him. Ken's dad tried to be encouraging and supportive by making learning fun, with jokes and stories. For some reason Ken couldn't learn. Ken was confused because, although he was trying, his reading remained poor and he knew his dad was unhappy.

Ken's dad wanted Ken to know the alphabet. He thought then Ken would be able to read properly. But Ken didn't know that he was supposed to be learning the alphabet. He thought he was supposed to be having fun with his dad. Ken's dad thought his son was lazy and dull.

Ken's dad had not realised Ken didn't know that the real purpose of their sessions together was learning to read. Once Ken did know what he was supposed to be doing, he began to learn. Ken's dad was then able to help effectively because he made clear throughout their sessions together:

♦ what he was going to teach

♦ how he was going to teach it

♦ when playtime stopped and started

♦ when lessons began

This raises the question: can learning be fun?

Yes! Learning can be fun if it is done in a supportive working environment which is protected. A protected working environment is one where you and your child know what you are trying to achieve. There will be a clear start and finish time. Interruptions will be kept to a minimum and dealt with rapidly and distractions will be removed. You teach your child to understand that because learning is important it requires time, attention and effort and the best environment for learning will be protected. By providing a protected environment for children when they are young, they will know how to create one for themselves when they are older.

The purpose of learning is to acquire more skills and understanding.

The best learning environment is relaxed, purposeful, comfortable and cheerful, with a noise level appropriate to the activities. Each person is able to go about their own business, individually or in groups, without disturbing others.

A GOOD LEARNING ENVIRONMENT IS CREATED BY:

THE ATTITUDE OF EVERYONE PARTICIPATING
AND A SENSE THAT THE PURPOSE IS KNOWN

RESPECT FOR THE EFFORT NEEDED TO WORK SUCCESSFULLY

RESPECT FOR THE LEARNING STYLES OF
INDIVIDUAL MEMBERS OF THE GROUP

FLEXIBILITY WHICH ALLOWS FOR INDIVIDUAL NEEDS TO BE MET

A BELIEF THAT THE TASK CAN BE ACCOMPLISHED

TIME BEING AVAILABLE TO DO THE WORK

NECESSARY RESOURCES BEING AVAILABLE

THE PHYSICAL STATE OF THE PARTICIPANTS

THE PHYSICAL ENVIRONMENT

AN UNDERSTANDING OF THE PURPOSE OF LEARNING

Helen felt learning at home was fun because her mum made her feel they were learning together. When homework was being done they would stop for a chat but both understood the work would continue until it was finished. Helen knew she would have the benefit of her mother's support when needed and also her companionship. Homework became a part of the fabric of the family life. Other family members, as they arrived home, were included in the chat or in the work.

ONE STEP AT A TIME

USE IT OR LOSE IT –
IS PRACTICE NECESSARY?

Some children appear to learn everything very quickly but nothing sticks

In some cases learning is more apparent than real. Sam gets a spelling list of five words every night. Every night he learns them and gets them right. But each new list seems to act as an eraser of the old list. Sam can only remember five words at a time and he can only remember them in the order he has learned them. He is memorising the shape and sequence of the letters. He doesn't know that the letters record sounds. He doesn't know once he's learnt his spellings he's supposed to use them. The spelling list is to give him the words to be able to write his own thoughts.

Learning something in the wrong way and for the wrong reasons can mean it will take a long time to unlearn it before being able to relearn it the right way. If parents and teachers don't recognise the time it will take, they can panic and think the child is of low ability or has a special learning difficulty, when in fact he has to spend a bit more time on learning a particular skill properly because he learned it the wrong way the first time.

Some children appear to learn everything very quickly but don't ever use it

Philippa paid attention, learned her spellings and would write interesting sentences using each of the words, but had not realised that her spelling list was meant to double as a vocabulary list. When writing her own stories, although she knew the meaning and could spell words like 'delightful', 'exhilarating', 'glorious' and 'pleasant', she would write 'It was a nice day and we had a nice time'.

Some children appear to learn everything very quickly but look for ways of avoiding doing what they have been asked

Thomas loves discussion. Any observer of a discussion in Thomas' class would see him as a very bright boy, with lots of ideas and able to answer all the questions. If the observer stayed and saw Thomas at his desk when the class was doing follow-up work, the impression of Thomas' ability would change dramatically as the observer would see Thomas doing very little.

Thomas is a child with aptitude but no application. This means he knows what to do but has no strategies for getting himself going. Even if helped to start, he stops the minute the help stops. He doesn't realise that he is supposed to be taking over. This means Thomas does not allow himself opportunities to have his real ability recognised by others.

In all of these examples the children have not understood the steps of learning. They often haven't even realised there are steps.

Some children appear to learn everything very quickly and others seem to take forever, but almost all children need time to learn. Those who pick up something quickly are often in danger of not being able to use it. They have missed the steps which give new learning its place in the structure, its power, its relevance and use.

The apprenticeship model of learning

The apprenticeship model of learning is important. If your child gets something wrong – whether it is speech, reading, writing or tidying a room – teach your child how to improve, how to do better and how to move on.

Remember, a mistake is an opportunity to learn for both your child and you!

Children used to lie or sit in a pram watching the adult's mouth move and practise getting their own mouths to make the same shape. Many children now are not given the opportunity to see how the mouth should move when a word is said because:

♦ they face away from the adult in a pram or stroller

♦ they eat alone rather than around a table with adults and other children

♦ they listen to bedtime stories on a tape rather than having an adult read it to them

♦ they are strapped into car seats which protect their safety but mean they can't see the mouth of the person talking

♦ the use of puppets on television and video means that spoken language is not associated with appropriate mouth shapes

♦ teaching careful enunciation to small children is ridiculed

Remember, children who can mimic a sound or do an exercise after they have been shown how, have not necessarily learned how to do it for themselves. Learning takes time.

Karen was learning to skip and her efforts were shared and encouraged by her granny who recognised the many skills involved in learning to skip. But Karen's aunt could only see her attempts at skipping as Karen having her feet flat on the floor and her shoulders going up and down.

Gradually Karen learnt new physical movements. Each one was noted, commented on and applauded by her granny. Karen was her grandmother's apprentice. She was given lots of encouragement, lots of help and lots of time to learn each new bit.

This method of teaching skipping is the same as the method which should be used for teaching clear speech.

How is it that YES is a four-letter word?

Radio announcers, television presenters and pop stars often use slang and vogue words which children soak up and accept as common usage, so children can't always understand why you should comment on their speech.

You are right to comment!

Believing that poor speech is good speech can damage children's development. If they think 'yes' is a two letter word 'ye', how will they know it is spelt as a three letter word, and how will they know that what they are actually saying is a four letter word, 'yeah'?

Your child needs to know about selecting and using language appropriate for different settings. Children who do not understand this are at a disadvantage.

If you have a relaxed way of speaking at home, practise reading anything out loud so your child can repeat what has just been said. Choose a short passage, read out a sentence each and then repeat it, trying to improve pronunciation and articulation each time. You can make it enjoyable by using different accents.

EDUCATION MATTERS

Sometimes you may be worried about how your child is getting on at school.

The school may be happy but you are unhappy: this can happen if your child is invisible at school. The school may have low expectations of your child and feel you are pushy.

The school is unhappy but you don't see anything to be worried about: you are happy with your child at home and don't understand why there is a problem at school. You don't recognise your child as the one the school is describing.

You feel the school is teaching the material, not your child: your child is finishing the work but you know it is not being understood.

Homework is a problem: your child isn't able to do homework because of not understanding what is supposed to be done. This can be because your child's listening skills are poor or the explanation from school was poor. Sometimes the instructions are not adequate for you to even know how to help!

Can't work, won't work: your child is refusing to do homework. This could be because your child finds school stressful and needs home to be a refuge, or because your child hasn't got the skills needed to complete the work. Your child may not do the work because of a lack of skills but, will not tell you, so it appears as though your child won't rather than can't. Stubbornness on the part of your child can make it hard for you to overcome your irritation long enough to find the real problem.

Slap and dash: your child rushes off homework and then claims to have done all that is required.

But the teacher said... : your child doesn't believe you will know how to satisfy the demands of the teacher.

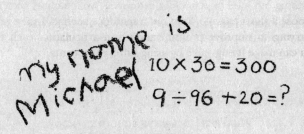

Ryan was a very good speller.

One night he had spellings to do. He was so insistent that:

> ♦ he had to do his spellings
>
> ♦ he had to do them in a special way
>
> ♦ it was going to be a difficult task
>
> ♦ any help from his mum might not be right, because he was worried she would not know what his teacher's special way was.

Eventually Ryan told his mum this extra special and very difficult spelling task was to learn two words, 'xylophone' and 'succeed'. The extra special way he had to learn them was to:

> ♦ look at them
>
> ♦ mark out the shape of them
>
> ♦ cover them over
>
> ♦ write them
>
> ♦ find any small words hidden in them

Ryan's mum was able to help him and this meant that next time Ryan had more trust in his mum.

If you are worried about anything to do with your child's life at school, you should get in touch with someone. It will be whoever you've been told is your first point of contact with the school. It may be the class teacher, year head, deputy head or head teacher. You may speak to the teachers by telephone, send a letter or make an appointment.

THE FOLLOWING QUESTIONS MAY HELP YOU TO GET YOUR THOUGHTS CLEAR BEFORE YOU CONTACT THE SCHOOL.

WHAT IS WORRYING ME?

WHY AM I CONCERNED?

DO I HAVE ANY EVIDENCE, SUCH AS A PIECE OF WORK?

WHAT DO I THINK THE SCHOOL CAN DO?

The more you have thought about what you want to say, the more likely you are to sort out the problem. Jot down your thoughts – they will help you remember everything you want to say at the meeting.

If you are nervous about going in to school, see if a friend can come with you. Make sure you have discussed the details with your friend before you go and your friend knows what you want him or her to do. It is a good idea to take notes while you are in a meeting so you have something to refer to later.

Preparing yourself like this for any meeting can help you put your case and hear what is being said.

CHAPTER 4

STAIRWAY TO SUCCESS

SKILLS FOR COPING WITH LIFE

SKILLS FOR COPING WITH LEARNING

SKILLS FOR ENJOYING LIFE

SKILLS FOR COPING WITH PEOPLE

SKILLS FOR THINKING

The A-Z for success

Adventure
Be relaxed
Common sense
Don't criticise
Experimenting
Fulfilling
Good working environment
Happiness
Information
Just be yourself
Knowledge
Listening
Making mistakes
Notes
Optimism
Practice
Questions
Risk taking
Support
Thinking
Unlimited potential
Value
Watching
eXplain
You don't have to be perfect...
...Zero doesn't mean nothing!

In the last chapter we talked about why children stumble, why they may feel or appear to be 'failures'. The truth is that we are all successful, but sometimes we don't believe it.

Remember, you and your child are learning together. You both learn best if you are comfortable, relaxed and thoughtful.

A Learning Home

A comfortable home is a learning home.

It may be tidy or untidy but it will need pencils and paper.

It may be large or small but it will need somewhere to work.

It may be crowded or empty but it will need a quiet space sometimes.

A relaxed home is a learning home.

Home is a refuge for everyone who lives there. It is everyone's protection against the busy and demanding world. It's a place to recoup, recover and recharge batteries. It will be relaxed if each person's needs are recognised and everyone knows how to negotiate and compromise for everybody's benefit.

A thoughtful home is a learning home.

Children who know that as family members they are expected to be responsible for certain jobs will learn what it is like to be a member of a community. These children will get practice in how to make decisions. They will realise that everything can't be done, that some things have to be left and that sometimes priorities change. They will realise that some days are busy and demanding and some are restful.

Climbing the stairway together

YOU AND YOUR CHILD WILL WANT TO CLIMB THE
STAIRWAY TO SUCCESS TOGETHER SO THAT YOUR CHILD:

♦ will always be able to cope with life, whether everything is
  going right or not
♦ can enjoy life
♦ will be fascinated by everything that's seen and everyone met
♦ sees life as an adventure
♦ treats people with respect
♦ is a good listener
♦ knows how to learn
♦ is not afraid of expressing beliefs
♦ is happy to help others
♦ asks and answers questions
♦ doesn't make assumptions but keeps an open mind
♦ doesn't expect to be right every time
♦ can make decisions

Once you have agreed this, you can get started!

SKILLS FOR COPING WITH LIFE

Choices

Whether life is going a child's way or not, the child needs to know
that there are choices, and that every time a decision is made
there will be a consequence.

IF JOSHUA CHOOSES TO LEAVE HIS HOMEWORK AND GO OUT
TO PLAY FOOTBALL INSTEAD, HE MIGHT HAVE A GOOD TIME
PLAYING FOOTBALL BUT THE NEXT DAY HE WON'T HAVE
ANY HOMEWORK TO HAND IN.

IF HE HELPS HIS BROTHER TIDY HIS ROOM THEN
EVERYONE FEELS HAPPY.

Coping skills are not about children getting adults to sort things out
or being given presents because they have sorted them out. Coping
skills are knowing how to sort things out for ourselves and seeing
the benefit of what we have done. Coping skills have to be taught.

Decisions

Once we realise that even if we are doing nothing we will be
making an impact, we can make better decisions.

IF EMILY IS SITTING QUIETLY IN THE CLASSROOM AND GETTING ON
WITH HER WORK WHEN THAT'S WHAT SHE'S SUPPOSED TO BE DOING,
THE TEACHER WILL NOTICE SHE CAN GET ON; EMILY WILL NOTICE
SHE'S GETTING THROUGH HER WORK AND HER FRIENDS WILL NOTICE
SHE'S SOMEONE WHO WANTS TO WORK.

IF EMILY IS SITTING QUIETLY AND GETTING ON WITH HER WORK
WHEN SHE'S SUPPOSED TO BE JOINING THE OTHERS IN A
DISCUSSION, THE TEACHER WILL FEEL SHE'S BEING DIFFICULT; SHE
WILL BE ISOLATED AND HER FRIENDS WILL FEEL SHE'S NOT SHARING.

Success in school means realising each of us is part of a supportive
community and the decisions we make should protect the chance
to learn for everyone.

Success at home means realising each of us is part of a
supportive community and the decisions we make will affect how
supported other people feel.

Keeping an open mind

A confident child will find it easy to keep an open mind and
simply observe differences while enjoying the unexpected. A
confident child will learn by reflecting on new information and
deciding where that new information might fit.

I know what I know

Children feel confident if they know that it's all right to be different and they don't have to follow the crowd. They will be happy to let other people have their own ideas.

As thinkers, children need to know why what they think is different to what others think. They will need to know that they are not alone just because they think differently – there are lots of things they can share, but it is not easy for anyone to find a 'best' friend.

Remember, people will like a child even when they don't share the same ideas or want to be the child's bosom buddy.

Skills for coping with learning

Boundaries are not barriers

A boundary helps us cope because it shows us what the system is. If a child knows that the playground is for playing in, while the classroom is for working in, that child will be able to learn more.

Children beginning life with similar talents and potential will develop differently. The child who knows about boundaries will learn more than the child who is left not knowing that if you want to get on there are things you can do and things you can't do.

Listen

Being a good listener is all about giving attention. Giving attention is about clearing a space in your mind so that you can hear what is being said.

Being a good listener is great preparation for being a good learner.

. . . and learn

For a child, knowing how learning happens is liberating. Once we realise that some things we learn without noticing, some things we learn easily and other things take time to learn, we can be relaxed about learning. We can be excited, not frightened, about learning something difficult.

Asking questions

If a child is happy to ask questions, it will be because the child has been allowed to ask questions and is interested in the answers. Show interest in what your child does and encourage questions about what you've been doing.

If you don't do something, nothing gets done

A child who 'has a go' knows it's better to do something rather than nothing.

> IN A MATHS CLASS MATTHEW KNOWS HE'S SUPPOSED
> TO BE DOING A PAGE OF SUMS BUT HE'S NOT SURE HOW,
> SO HE DOES ONE AND THEN HAS IT CHECKED.
>
> HE'S GIVEN THE TEACHER A CHANCE TO TEACH HIM
> AND HE'S GIVEN HIMSELF A CHANCE TO LEARN.

> IN A MATHS CLASS ERIC KNOWS HE'S SUPPOSED TO
> BE DOING THE PAGE OF SUMS BUT HE'S NOT SURE HOW,
> SO HE ONLY WRITES THE DATE.
>
> HE'S ONLY LET THE TEACHER KNOW THAT HE HASN'T
> DONE THE WORK. SHE DOESN'T KNOW WHY AND SHE DOESN'T
> KNOW HOW SHE CAN HELP HIM. HE'S LOST THE OPPORTUNITY
> TO BE TAUGHT AND SO HAS LOST THE OPPORTUNITY TO LEARN.

SKILLS FOR ENJOYING LIFE

A child who enjoys life is someone who recognises the good in the current situation and isn't always clamouring to do something else.

Strange as it may sound, some children have to learn to enjoy things.

> PAUL WAS 8 AND NEVER HAPPY. HE ALWAYS ASKED IF HE COULD
> DO SOMETHING ELSE. AS SOON AS HE STARTED DOING SOMETHING
> NEW HE WOULD ASK TO CHANGE. HE WAS FRANTIC AS HE TRIED
> TO HAVE EVERYTHING AT THE SAME TIME AND FELT THAT
> WHAT HE REALLY WANTED HE STILL WASN'T DOING.

PAUL LEARNED TO THINK ABOUT WHAT HE WANTED AND MAKE CHOICES ABOUT WHAT HE WAS GOING TO HAVE. HE BEGAN TO REALISE THAT HE WAS GETTING ENJOYMENT BY LETTING GO. HE FOUND THAT IT WAS POSSIBLE TO ENJOY HIMSELF ONCE HE CONCENTRATED ON WHAT HE WAS DOING AND STOPPED WORRYING ABOUT WHAT HE WAS MISSING.

Because it's fascinating . . .

For children who are fascinated by what they see, what they do and who they meet, the possibilities are endless. They will be able to learn from every situation. They will always be adding to their store of knowledge. They will see the excitement in life.

Don't expect always to share the same fascination as your child and don't expect your child to share yours. It's lovely if it does happen, but it can't be forced. Better to let your child discover the enjoyment of life for himself or herself, and make it possible – within reason – wherever your support is needed.

. . . and full of adventures

There's no piece of information an adventurous child doesn't use in some way. It may be used immediately, it might appear in a story years later or it might be another piece in a puzzle the child will learn to understand.

A child who sees life as an adventure builds up an enormous reservoir of experiences that can be drawn on in all sorts of situations.

Skills for coping with people

Being a people person

By learning to see others for who they are and not what they look like or what they've got, we discover who we are. We know sometimes we're right and sometimes we're wrong, sometimes we're happy and sometimes we're sad, sometimes we're outgoing and sometimes we're shy. A child who has learned this will not feel the need for a particular make of shoe or a particular make of bag to be likeable to people who really matter.

Helping

Being willing to help shows that a child is sensitive to others. To help well, the child needs to be looking, listening, thinking and asking questions. The child must realise that there are other people in the world.

SKILLS FOR THINKING

Your child will be thinking all day – maybe not about things you'd like, but certainly thinking!

A CHILD WHO LEARNS HOW TO DEVELOP THINKING WILL BE MORE SUCCESSFUL.

Activities for developing thinking

OBSERVATIONS

THIS IS A JOINT EXERCISE TO INCREASE THE SCOPE OF POSSIBLE ANSWERS. IT CAN BE DONE BETWEEN YOU AND THE CHILD OR IN A GROUP OF ANY NUMBER.

1. Take any object – toy, item of clothing, ornament. Here we're using a vase of flowers.

2. Give the child paper and pencil.

3. Say that you both have a minute to write down what can be seen. If your child is hesitant, suggest thinking about colour, shape, number, material.

4. Take it in turns to share your ideas and write them down on a new piece of paper so you can both see them. The vase of flowers – 10 flowers, vase, two kinds, water, purple, soft, standing, delicate, dying.

5. Decide what you're going to do next.

YOU COULD CONTINUE AS A MATHS SESSION BY:

♦ counting all the leaves

♦ working out ways of measuring the volume of the vase

♦ finding shapes in the flowers

♦ discussing symmetry

♦ making patterns

♦ devising sums, e.g. 3 white flowers + 7 purple = 10 flowers

YOU COULD CONTINUE AS A LANGUAGE SESSION BY:

♦ working on detailed descriptions of differences and similarities, e.g. long narrow leaves and short, fat vase

♦ using a thesaurus to find out more ways of describing the petals, the stem or the vase

♦ using an encyclopaedia to find words connected with flowers, e.g. pistil, stamen, bulb, root

You COULD CONTINUE AS A STORY SESSION BY THINKING OF HOW FLOWERS MIGHT APPEAR IN A STORY. THEY COULD APPEAR BECAUSE THEY WERE:

♦ a present

♦ seen on a walk through a beautiful garden

♦ sent through the post

♦ in a shopping basket

♦ grown from seed which you found in a tin when you were in your grandfather's shed. He couldn't remember what they were but felt they might have come from his distant cousin who lived on a tiny coral island with only his parrot for company ... see what happens when you start thinking of ideas!

You could think about the senses and how you use each sense to add to the information you can collect, e.g. The flower smells peppery, the petals feel cool and velvety.

The more detail children take in from the world around them, the more avenues they will have to explore. Their thinking will be wider, deeper and diverse.

MINIMISE TO MAXIMISE

THIS IS A TECHNIQUE FOR DEVELOPING THE ABILITY TO THINK WIDELY ABOUT WHAT SEEMS VERY NARROW.

1. Take any word and ask your child to give you any ideas or words to do with the original word. Put your ideas down too. The word could be water.

2. In one minute it is possible for two people to think of more than twenty words.

drought	splash	shower	pipe	pond
drip	drop	drink	glass	rain
pollution	swimming	reservoir	pool	water the garden
river	damp	flood	bath	sea
soggy	roots	washing	liquid	soap
drain	bucket	puddle	leak	irrigation
dam	waves	clouds	spring	sparkling

3. Now put the words on separate pieces of paper.

4. Can you think of ways to group the words?

♦ words to do with farming

♦ words to do with weather

♦ words to do with water systems

♦ noises

♦ containers

♦ bodies of water

♦ effects of water

♦ things that need water

If a word fits into more than one group then make an extra slip of paper with that word.

5. Now see if you can build each group up so that it has twenty words in it.

CONTAINERS:

bath	sink	bubbler	trough	reservoir
fountain	dam	jug	saucepan	glass
cooler	bucket	bottle	tank	vase
radiator	bowl	flask	barrel	decanter

6. You could try subdividing some of those lists.

♦ kitchen containers

♦ garden containers

♦ containers you can drink from

♦ bathroom containers

By taking something so simple and discovering how much there is to say about it, your child will realise that any word can spark off a thousand thoughts. From a thousand thoughts your child can choose just one to think about, which can lead to thousands more!

THIS IS A WAY OF EXPLAINING WHAT YOU'RE THINKING AND
THINKING WHILE YOU'RE DOING!

ASK YOUR CHILD TO TELL YOU HOW TO DRAW A SQUARE, USING
WORDS ONLY – NO HANDS TO DEMONSTRATE OR DESCRIBE.

THIS IS THE WAY IT USUALLY GOES.

1. Draw four lines.

You don't know in which direction the lines should go
(horizontal, vertical, diagonal).

You don't know if the lines are to be joined or how long
each line should be.

Don't say what your child hasn't told you, just draw what
your child says and then invite another go.

2. Draw four lines that meet at the corner.

You still don't know about the right angles, equal lines or
direction.

3. Draw four equal lines which meet at right angles to form a closed
   shape.

If your child doesn't mention that the shape has to be closed you could still come up with something like the image above. This exercise can be amusing for you both.

It may take many steps before your child manages to tell you enough for you to draw it accurately.

COMPARE AND CONTRAST

THIS IS A WAY TO MAKE YOUR CHILD MORE AWARE OF ALL THE DIFFERENCES THERE ARE IN THINGS THAT SEEM THE SAME AND ALL THE SIMILARITIES THERE ARE IN THINGS THAT SEEM DIFFERENT.

1. Take a stool and a chair.
2. Get your child to note down everything about them.

STOOL	CHAIR
seat	seat
3 legs	4 legs
no back	back
padded	hard
circular seat	four sided seat
30 centimetres from the floor to the seat	35 centimetres from the floor to the seat
no extra supports	support struts for the legs
study	kitchen
light	heavy

3. Now list the things which are different. Your child may want to add new things as they come to mind.

- ◆ colour
- ◆ size
- ◆ material
- ◆ shape
- ◆ number of legs
- ◆ back
- ◆ comfort
- ◆ use
- ◆ construction

And then the things which are the same:

- ◆ seat
- ◆ legs
- ◆ used in the house
- ◆ manufactured
- ◆ bought at the same shop
- ◆ used for sitting
- ◆ can be used for reaching things down off the shelf

4. Get your child to put some of the information into sentences to explain how the two objects appear.

ALTHOUGH BOTH OF THEM ARE PIECES OF FURNITURE USED FOR SITTING, ONE HAS A BACK AND THE OTHER DOES NOT.

ALTHOUGH THEY ARE BOTH FOR SITTING, ONLY ONE OF THEM IS COMFORTABLE.

This can lead on to further discussion about personal preference which could end up with:

I LIKE SITTING ON THE STOOL BECAUSE IT HAS A SOFT SEAT BUT I FIND THE CHAIR UNCOMFORTABLE BECAUSE IT HAS A HARD SEAT.

This method teaches a child to express likes and dislikes or what is known and not known.

... people are fascinating

A child on the 'stairway to success' will be comfortable with his own strengths and happy to work on his own weaknesses.

He will understand that he is an individual as well as a member of many groups. He will enjoy living in a world with so many different people and be fascinated by the different ways other people see the world in which they live. He will be able to make connections with other people.

He will be happy to cooperate and work with others or work alone. Because he will know how he learns best, the learning he does will be focused and purposeful.

... learning is a chance to discover new possibilities

This child will understand that his knowledge is unlimited and so are his horizons — he will never stop learning. New learning becomes possible because he knows any problem can be broken down into parts small enough for him to cope with. As he learns he will know how to look for connections between the things he learns and the things he knows.

He will be relaxed about mistakes, whether they are his or someone else's, because he will see them as a chance to find out more.

He will practise at skills until he gets better and will love asking questions and listening to the answers.

... love is everywhere

This child will appreciate the love and care of his family. He will realise lots of people have the same feelings as he has.

. . . *safety is the key*

This child will understand how events happen. He will know events have causes, whether the causes are understood or not. He will know that there are effects after an event, although some may happen immediately and some take time to become apparent.

He will know his body, mind, heart and spirit matter and he should care for them. He will try not to harm anyone else. He will think about the consequences of his own actions and be aware of the consequences of what others do.

. . . *the world is vulnerable*

He will take responsibility for protecting his environment and the people in it. He will be concerned about the world around him and what he can do to improve it.

. . . *new horizons beckon*

He will be excited by change and see the possibilities. He will develop his imagination. He will become able to plan and organise as he goes.

. . . *peace is perfect*

He will know how to cope with the challenges of life. He will know how to reach his point of peace. He will be able to use words to express his feelings and thoughts. He will enjoy the little things as well as the big things.

CHAPTER 5

CREATING KIDS WHO CAN SPELL

How to teach the alphabet

Help! My Child Can't Spell

The Magic Spell

Getting started: 10 simple steps

Moving on

Righting wrongs

Exercises and games

The difference between good spellers and bad spellers is that good spellers know when they can spell the word, and when they are not sure they get help from someone else or a dictionary. Bad spellers think that spelling is a mystery which cannot be unravelled. Good spellers know that spelling is an intriguing mystery.

HOW TO TEACH THE ALPHABET

You can start teaching your child the alphabet when you think he or she is ready. This might be as early as three if your child is showing interest. If your child does not show any interest by five, you can gently introduce learning the letters in the alphabet sequence. Your child may only learn two or three letters in sequence in the beginning, but don't panic and don't give up.

AS THEY LEARN THE ALPHABET, CHILDREN UNDERSTAND THAT:

THE ALPHABET IS MADE UP OF LETTERS

THE LETTERS HAVE SOUNDS AND NAMES

THERE ARE 26 LETTERS AND THEY HAVE A PARTICULAR ORDER

THE CHILDREN'S OWN NAMES ARE WRITTEN WITH
SOME OF THOSE LETTERS

Knowing the alphabet will help children use a dictionary to find out more words when they need them.

Ideas for teaching the alphabet

1. Let your child see you use the alphabet, for example in an address book, telephone book or index.
2. Ask your child to write any letters he or she knows. Then get your child to find out what letter comes before and after. Number the letters your child has written in the alphabet: a=1, b=2, z=26.
3. To encourage the learning of more letters in sequence, get your child to write down as many letters as possible in order, starting with 'a'. Whenever your child is unable to write the next letter, you write it and then your child tries the sequence again. For example, your child

writes 'a, b, c, d, e, f'. You add a 'g'. Then your child writes the sequence again with the new addition. When your child can write the sequence from memory, add a new letter. Stick to either capital letters or lower case letters when you are first teaching; introduce the other case when your child is secure.

4. Ask your child to tell you the sounds. Make sure each sound is said clearly when your child points to the letter. Some letters are notoriously difficult for small children, such as 'r' and 'w'. Different letters will present a problem for different children, but persist in getting your child to say letters clearly because this is an important skill for successful spelling. Ask your child to tell you letter names. If he or she doesn't know the names for certain letters, persist in teaching them but don't panic. 'I Spy' is a good game to make letter names fun.

5. Once children know their letters they can think about where they come in relation to each other. Number the letters 1-26 and ask your child to write his or her name using numbers. For example, Adam is 1,4,1,14. Now ask your child to decide which letters go in the first half of the alphabet and which into the second. This will help your child increase speed when using the dictionary. Knowing the alphabet and where the letters come gives children a tool for dictionary work, even if they only know the first two letters of a word.

HELP! MY CHILD CAN'T SPELL!

Don't panic! All that has happened is that your child has not been taught in the way he learns. There are many possible reasons for this. Children with spelling problems may:

♦ have hearing problems

♦ have speech problems

♦ have sight problems

♦ have been ill and missed school when it mattered

♦ be the youngest in the class

♦ have thought spelling was easy and didn't need any effort

♦ have thought they couldn't learn

♦ have linked the wrong letter shape to the sound

♦ be unable to write each letter accurately

- have had a series of teachers in a short space of time
- have not been taught in their strongest language
- have not been taught to spell
- have been diagnosed by experts as being unable to learn

Spelling is a matter of confidence. Poor spellers, once they've become confident, will be happy to think about spelling. Spelling is a thinking activity.

Ingredients for a good spell

LEARNING TO SPELL CAN BE FUN

GOOD SPELLING IS NOT GENETIC

SPELLCHECKS ARE NOT FOOLPROOF – THEY WON'T
TELL YOU WHICH WITCH TO USE

SPEAKING CLEARLY MEANS YOU'RE MORE THAN HALFWAY THERE

SUCCESS BREEDS SUCCESS – DON'T BECOME SPELLBOUND

GET THE TWO AND THREE LETTER WORDS RIGHT AND YOU'LL BE
ABLE TO SPELL WORDS WITH FOUR, FIVE AND MORE LETTERS

YOU MIGHT ALREADY BE A GOOD SPELLER – IF YOU JUST
TIDIED UP YOUR HANDWRITING SO PEOPLE COULD
READ WHAT YOU HAD WRITTEN!

COPYING IS NOT A CRIME

MAKE IT MANAGEABLE – BREAK IT UP INTO LITTLE BITS

REMEMBER THAT RHYME – YOU'LL USE IT IN TIME

PHONICS ARE FOREVER

USE IT OR LOSE IT – SO WRITE IT!

aBCDe

Bite size pieces

Do not start by only teaching your child spelling rules – children who learn to observe will gradually understand the system. The important thing to remember is that we learn to spell by thinking. We think best if we focus our attention on what is in front of us on the page.

If we know that:

♦ the alphabet is made up of two kinds of letters – vowels and consonants

♦ letters are combined in different ways to make words

then we are able to spell.

ALL BIG WORDS ARE MADE UP OF SYLLABLES.

ALL SYLLABLES ARE SOUND BITES.

SOME SYLLABLES ARE LITTLE WORDS.

EVERY SYLLABLE HAS A VOWEL.

un + der = under   TWO SOUND BITES MAKE 'under'

can + not = cannot   TWO LITTLE WORDS MAKE 'cannot'

When looking at a word, we need to look for:

♦ THE VOWELS – THEY ARE 'a', 'e', 'i', 'o', 'u' AND SOMETIMES 'y' IN WORDS LIKE 'baby' AND 'hymn'

♦ THE SOUND BITE OR THE LITTLE WORD THAT THE VOWEL IS A PART OF

Sometimes we find that the vowel is a syllable all on its own

man / u / fac / ture

Sometimes we find that a vowel is not spoken

heat / ing	THE 'a' IS SILENT
same	THE 'e' IS SILENT

Knowing common sound bites can make spelling and reading easier. The common sound bites are:

er	ir	or	ur	ly	be	ing	a	ar
est	ous	re	de	com	im	en	ex	ed
mis	y	dis	pre	un	age	ful	ment	con

In some cases one letter name is made from two letters

be = b, ex = x, en = n, ar = r.

Knowing how letters make their own names in a word can make spelling and reading easier. This can help children overcome misunderstandings about how words are formed.

Remember, you are trying to take the fear out of the word and leave in the excitement of the challenge.

THE MAGIC SPELL

The Magic Spell shows children that they can spell – and quite long words too! It is a quick, sure-fire way of building self-confidence while making children interested in spelling.

When we use this, the first thing we always say is: 'The person being tested is me. You are here to find out whether I'm any good and whether I can help you'. We suggest you do the same thing. Explain to your child that you are both going to check whether this method works.

How to cast the Magic Spell

1. Ask your child to find a word to try out. It can be any word. Your child doesn't have to be able to read it, just point to it.

2. Then your child can read out the letters to you.

3. Write the word out so that your child can see it.

4. Now ask what your child can see when looking at the word, and say what you can see.

5. Write down what you've both said you can see.

6. Now, if you haven't already noticed, look to see whether there are any double letters or letters repeated. See *What can you see in a word?* on page 97.

7. Now see if your child can spell the word out loud.

8. If so, see if he or she can spell it backwards.

9. If not, see where the mistake is being made and offer suggestions for how to memorise the word. See *How to memorise a word* on page 98.

10. Now, try Step 7 again.

The Magic Spell works because children realise they can memorise words which they thought were too hard. When they thought they were stupid or couldn't spell, their energy was used up worrying, feeling frightened or helpless because they knew they wouldn't be able to hide the fact. After using the Magic Spell, their energy can be directed into learning spelling successfully. Instead of believing they can't, they now believe they can!

How it works

1. **What happens when a child chooses the word?** When a child is allowed to choose the word he has maximum control. If he's feeling frightened he may choose a simple word with few letters, such as 'cat'. Go through the steps, but as soon as he wants to spell it out to you, let

him – both forwards and backwards. He will then feel excited about finding the next word to try. It might be four letters or it might be 14.

2 **What happens when he reads the letters out loud?** When he reads the letters out loud to you, you'll know whether he is saying the letters clearly enough for him to be able to use them in spelling. You will know whether he knows all the letters in the word. You will know whether he is confused about any of the letters in the word, and you can help him to sort out the confusion.

3. **What happens when he writes down the word?** By writing down the word as he tells you the letters, he is able to see the sounds he is making turned into letter shapes. You are still not making any demands on him, he is in control of the pacing and because you are writing it for him, he is free to concentrate on the spelling.

4. **What happens when he's asked what he can see?** People who can't spell usually haven't realised that there is anything to see. Sometimes a child sees a string of letters, sometimes a muddle of letters and sometimes just a problem. When your child realises you see lots of things in the word, he will realise that there is something to see and there is something to think about.

5. **What happens when the ideas are written down?** When you write down what you have both seen, it gives him two opportunities for remembering the word because he will be listening as well as looking. This will help keep his attention. It will also help you see more clearly what he understands and where he still needs help.

6. **What's the point of asking him questions?** If he is having trouble getting started you can ask him some questions. (See *What can you see in a word?* on page 97.) When you write down the answers, he's got even more information about the word as well as ideas for how he will memorise it. His observation will improve and he will be learning techniques that will help him when he comes to spell other words.

7. **Why does he have to spell the word out loud?** By asking him to spell the word out loud you are giving him the opportunity to demonstrate his skill. The skills needed to write a word are different to those for sounding it out, so don't try to mix the two here.

8. **What's the point of spelling the word backwards?** By asking him to spell the word backwards you are checking whether he has grasped all the letters. It makes the 'spell' even more wondrous for him because, if it was beyond belief that he could spell the word at all, it is magical to him that he has now become a speller beyond his wildest dreams.

9. **What's the benefit of making mistakes?** Every mistake tells you and him more about where he needs extra help: pronunciation, letter shapes, sounds and names, saying the word to himself as he spells it, realising you have to look at what you're doing and put effort into learning it.

10. **Why is it important to finish feeling a success?** It's always important to leave a spelling session with him feeling successful. Sometimes children are so excited by how much they can remember that they choose longer and longer words and will need more support to remember them. If your child learns how to fly when he's confident and how to accept support when he's not, the distance he flies will increase.

If it hasn't worked for you, see *Righting wrongs* on page 94.

GETTING STARTED: 10 SIMPLE STEPS

1. Teach your child the letter sounds.
2. Teach your child the letter names.
3. Teach your child to recognise the letter shapes.
   - ~ foam letter shapes in the bath
   - ~ magnetic letter shapes on the fridge
   - ~ pick out initial letters on advertisements
4. Teach him to make the letter shapes.
   - ~ make them out of plasticine
   - ~ draw them in the sand
   - ~ draw them on a blackboard
   - ~ trace them in the air with a finger
5. Teach your child to say the letter sound clearly.
6. Teach your child to say the letter name clearly.
7. Point out that letters are all around. Show your child letters from his or her name in other words.
8. Teach your child to make his or her own name using the letters.
9. Teach your child the alphabet song, pointing to the letters while singing.
10. Play 'I Spy' so that your child links the first sound to the letter that begins the word.

Robert sang the alphabet song but did not realise it had anything to do with the letters he was being taught. When he realised that, he made the connection between the letters and their names by pointing to the letters as he sang the song. Once he realised letters had sounds and names, he realised they could be used to make words and he began to spell.

MOVING ON

1. See *How to teach the alphabet* at the beginning of this chapter and choose where your child is up to and where you can go to next.

2. Teach the one-letter words 'I' and 'a'. This may sound silly, but even secondary school children can get them wrong.

3. Teach the following two-letter words which are simple because they are spelt the way they are spoken.

at	be	go	he	if	me	no	on	so
an	as	am	up	us	it	in	is	of	we

4. Teach the following two-letter words which are harder because they are not written the way they are spoken.

   by   do   my   to   or

   The benefits of learning the two-letter words and later the three-letter words are:

   ♦ with 25 two-letter words a child has the building blocks for many, many more

   ♦ a child can be introduced to syllables and shown that they are parts of words: 'into' has two syllables – 'in' and 'to'

   ♦ complicated words are less frightening once the child sees the two-letter words in them.

5. Now see how many three-letter words your child can make from the two-letter words he or she knows already.

   at   cat   bat   rat   fat

   You can use a book to find more words, such as 'ate'. These words could be written into an exercise book with at least 26 pages – each letter with its own page.

6. Introduce the harder three-letter words your child will need.

you	the	she	her	ask	may	two	one	too	all	put
any	are	our	who	how	why	was	saw	out	ear	

But don't forget that two-letter words matter too! Children race ahead once they know the two-letter words. They're the building blocks for spelling.

How to develop your child's spelling

When children can get 10/10 in every spelling test and write essays and stories with almost no spelling mistakes, they may appear to have 'cracked it'. But really they may be on a plateau and not reaching their potential.

What we want is that they:

♦ want to know more

♦ are excited about how words are spelt

♦ feel relaxed and see spelling in a foreign language as combinations of letters

♦ are confident about using a dictionary

♦ use a thesaurus to expand their vocabulary

♦ can use specialist dictionaries

♦ see the 'root' word in a word, together with the prefixes and suffixes that are added to it

♦ feel confident they can learn to spell the words they need

♦ know that when they meet a spelling difficulty they can cope

Here are three suggestions for developing a child's spelling.

INCREASE VOCABULARY

Find ten difficult words from a newspaper. Find out the meanings and, using the Magic Spell, see if your child can spell them forwards and backwards.

MAKE WRITING A CHALLENGE

Use a thesaurus to find words which could replace 'nice' in the following sentences.

It was a nice day.

I got a nice present.

I have just finished a nice book.

She had a nice face.

TACKLE ETYMOLOGY!

Develop the child's interest in where words come from – etymology. Etymological dictionaries explain how words originate, where they have come from and how their meaning has changed.

For example, 'punctuation' comes from 'puncture', meaning to make small holes which is what punctuation does to sentences!

RIGHTING WRONGS

THE GIRL WHO WROTE GOBBLEDY GOOK

When Lisa was 7 she wrote charming stories which she read aloud. When others tried to read them, all they could see was what appeared to be gobbledy gook. In Lisa's mind her sentence would say, 'I went to the park with my sister to play', but to the reader it was 'I sire bl the hop we may shp on yet'.

Needless to say, adults who tried to read it were puzzled!

Lisa was even more puzzled because she thought writing her ideas down meant she had to write a cluster of letters from the alphabet for each word and then remember what she wanted to say!

If you come across a speller like Lisa, you will probably have found somebody who has been busy learning – but the wrong thing. Lisa became stuck at a very early stage of learning to spell, rather like the small child who, brimming with confidence, reads you a make-believe story from a book. Lisa's problem was that she didn't realise she was pretend spelling.

What you can do to help a 'pretend speller'

1. Take a deep breath.

2. Check that the child can manage all the steps in *Getting Started* on page 91.

3. Give time to learn. Children who have learnt something wrongly will take longer to unlearn and relearn than if they learnt it correctly the first time.

4. See yourself and your child as a team which will experiment with ways of overcoming the problem, and make sure your child shares this view.

   In Lisa's case the techniques we found successful were going back through the alphabet making sure she had the sounds, and then making sure she could match the sounds to the letters and could write the letters properly.

From our experience helping children, especially if they have misunderstood what they should have been doing for some time, our advice is:

♦ Stay optimistic: no matter how many apparent setbacks there are, they will be gaining ground gradually.

♦ Keep teaching for the future, at the frontier of a child's knowledge. This will be a struggle, and the child will need constant support to keep from sliding.

♦ Keep exploring the things they know so they will know them better.

♦ Keep teaching the things they nearly know so they will really know them.

♦ Above all, keep smiling and reassuring yourself and your child by noticing what your child has learnt and what you've learnt about how to help. Don't give up!

THE BOY WHO WOULDN'T WRITE ANYTHING

David was 10 and whenever he had to write he would blush and wriggle. If pressed he would draw lots of lines. He would copy a word to show that he was not being defiant, but he couldn't spell at all and he didn't know how to ask how a word was spelt.

What you can do to help a child who writes very little and can't spell at all

1. Check that the child can manage all the steps in *Getting Started* on page 91.

2. Help build the child's confidence. Show how words which are written down can be used. This helps the child to feel that words are within his or her power, rather than feeling overpowered by words.

3. From one page of a book identify words and get your child to copy them down, putting them in lists according to the number of letters in each word.

> The dog ran across the road. Tim ran after him.
> A car came down the road. The car stopped. A man
> got out. 'You must not run across the road', he said.

1	2	3	4	5+
A	he	the	road	across
		dog	down	stopped
		ran		after
		Tim		
		car		

4. Now ask your child to write a sentence using the words. Your child will feel confident and delight in the ability to use the words to express thoughts so that someone else can read them. It doesn't matter if your child only uses the words that have been copied. As confidence develops, your child will begin to remember some words and want new ones. Being more confident will make your child open to new learning.

Children will become independent spellers gradually as they are trained to:

♦ look for the correct spelling of words in a book or dictionary

♦ attempt to spell a word when it is needed

♦ experiment on a piece of scrap paper before putting work into an exercise book

When influential people say something doesn't matter, immature people may believe them. So when a footballer or a pop star says: 'I never bothered at school. I can't spell for toffee and it's never stopped me', we get a Lewis.

Thousands of children, including Lewis, see working hard at football rather than putting effort into learning to spell as a sensible use of their time. The problem is that because being unable to spell or read has been labelled as a 'Special Learning Difficulty', Lewis' failure to learn to spell is accepted and pressure is taken off him.

Experts have encouraged his parents to make Lewis feel good about himself. So, when Lewis' friends are doing homework Lewis will be practising football. Lewis' spelling is never corrected in case he is discouraged, so he is trapped.

In contrast, in the football team he is expected to work on all his weaknesses. The game will not be adjusted to accommodate them. Lewis knows if he wants to do well at football he has to train, practice, recognise his weaknesses and do something about them.

Lewis gets sympathetic responses to his weaknesses in football but he gets simply apathetic responses to his weakness at spelling.

EXERCISES AND GAMES

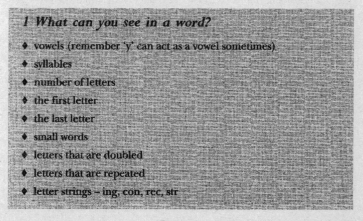

1 What can you see in a word?

- vowels (remember 'y' can act as a vowel sometimes)
- syllables
- number of letters
- the first letter
- the last letter
- small words
- letters that are doubled
- letters that are repeated
- letter strings – ing, con, rec, str

- confusing bits in the word
- shape
- silent letters
- spelling rules ('q' is always followed by a 'u' except in Qantas)
- mnemonics
- the number of letters in each syllable
- whether more than one syllable begins with the same letter
- whether the letters are saying their sounds or using another letter's sound – in 'circle' the first 'c' says 's' and the second 'c' says 'k'.

Looking at a word using the above suggestions shows how thinking can help you to learn a word accurately.

2 How to memorise a word

This is all about finding a way to remember the word. Just as we all work out our own way to remember our PIN number, we need to have a way of recalling words when we want to spell them. Your child might decide to:

- Look at the shape of the word.
- File away the word according to which list it is in – 'letter' would go in the double 't' list and in the list of words that end in 'er'.
- Use a mnemonic for the word :

'One collar and two sleeves' WILL HELP YOU TO REMEMBER THE NUMBER OF 'c'S AND 's'S IN 'necessary'.

'Bees eggs are ugly' TO REMEMBER THE ORDER OF THE FIRST (AND HARDEST) LETTERS IN 'beautiful'.

'Captain Cake risks ridicule' HELPS WITH THE SPELLING OF 'occurred'.

'Captain Cake makes mistakes' SORTS OUT 'accommodation'.

'Because' BECOMES EASIER ONCE YOU REMEMBER THAT 'use' COMES AT THE END.

'I hear with my ear' SORTS OUT THE CONFUSION OVER
WHEN TO USE 'here' AND WHEN TO USE 'hear'.

'Wear the earring' GIVES A CLUE ABOUT 'where' AND 'wear'.

'Their heirs will be rich' SHOWS WHICH
'their' SHOWS BELONGING.

'I saw him here, I saw him there and now I see him
everywhere' SHOWS THAT 'here' IS IN 'where' AND 'there' –
AND THEY ARE ALL ABOUT PLACES.

♦ Remember letters that have to be in the word – there is a 'u' in biscuit.

♦ Make links between that word and others – remember 'sign' by thinking of 'signal'.

♦ Remember the number of letters in the word – 'went' and 'when' are both four-letter words.

♦ Remember not all of the letters in a word are sounded – write, knee.

♦ Remember some of the letters in the word have different sounds than expected – bridge.

♦ Remember the little things that help a child recall the word – it starts with the same letter as the baby's name, or 'was' is 'saw' backwards.

Remember! What is being learnt must be clearly written and correct.

3 Anagrams

These give you loads of opportunities for thinking about spelling. A simple one ...

MAKE A LIST OF PARTS OF THE BODY:

   neck   foot   toe   leg   hand   skin   hip

NOW MUDDLE UP THE LETTERS SO THEY BECOME:

   knec   otof   eto   gel   nahd   knsi   phi

NOW SEE IF YOUR CHILD CAN UNMUDDLE THE WORDS.
A BIT HARDER ...

fist   knee   arm   elbow   hair   nose   ear

HARDER STILL ...

blood   vein   wrist   ankle   shoulder   thigh

NOW IT'S YOUR TURN ...

rebrevtea   poseoghaus   nosslit   streeria

... HARD ISN'T IT!

4 Wordsearches

Keep an empty grid handy for wordsearches and every spelling
list can become a game.

h	e	a	d	e	r	e	a	d	q
t	h	w	e	a	l	t	h	i	u
s	t	e	a	l	t	h	b	c	k
p	j	s	t	e	a	d	y	w	t
r	x	o	h	e	a	t	h	e	r
e	b	r	e	a	d	f	e	a	e
a	r	l	u	m	p	r	a	t	a
d	e	e	e	v	e	e	l	h	d
d	a	a	r	o	d	a	t	e	t
e	h	d	r	e	a	d	h	r	h

bread
dead
dread
head
health
heather
lead
leather
read
spread
steady
stealth
tread
wealth
weather

5 Word crosses

Help your child to see what's in a word. Find two words that have the same number of letters (it has to be an odd number). The middle letter has to be the same in both words.

BIG AND PIG

	p	
b	i	g
	g	

QUITE AND QUIET

	q		
	u		
q	u	i	t	e
	e		
	t		

6 My aunt likes...

This is a way of getting children to think about words and is ideal for long car journeys. Decide what it is your aunt likes. Let's say it's words with a double letter. Keep that to yourself and think of an example of something she likes and something she doesn't like.

My aunt likes coffee but she doesn't like tea.

The others playing the game have to think about what you've said and if anyone thinks they know what your aunt likes, they have to give an example too. If it's correct, they can say one for the rest of the group. If it's wrong, they have to keep thinking while you give more examples.

This game can become quite sophisticated if you choose two letters which can be confused, such as the first letters in 'cake' and 'kangaroo'.

My aunt likes kittens but she doesn't like cats.

My aunt likes kicking but she hates catching.

My aunt likes keeping things but she
doesn't like collections.

It can become even harder if the letter can appear anywhere in the word

My aunt likes donkeys but she doesn't like camels.

My aunt likes kids but she doesn't like uncles.

My aunt likes ankles but she doesn't like calves.

7 Running jumble

Even the simplest sentences can look odd without any spaces left between words. See if you can make this make sense.

Igotupthismorningandwashedmyface.

GETTING HARDER?

Iftheteaisnotonthetablethefamilywillbehungry.

NOW TRY THIS...

Scientistsworkingreatinstitutionscalleduniversities.

CHAPTER 6

CREATING KIDS WHO CAN READ

CREATING A BOOKWORM

ROUTES TO SUCCESSFUL READING

MAKING READING MORE MANAGEABLE

SUPPORTING A CHILD FROM COCOON TO FLIGHT

COMPLEX SENTENCES

OVERCOMING COMMON PROBLEMS

The A-Z of successful reading

CHILDREN WILL BECOME CONFIDENT
AND COMPETENT READERS IF:

THEIR PARENTS FEEL RELAXED ABOUT THEIR **A**BILITY TO HELP

THEY ARE GIVEN **B**OOKS WHICH THEY FIND INTERESTING
AND ATTRACTIVE

THEY SEE BOOKS AT HOME AND HAVE THEIR OWN **C**OLLECTIONS

THEY **D**ON'T HAVE TO START AT THE BEGINNING OR
FINISH AT THE END OF A BOOK

THEY RECOGNISE READING AS SOMETHING THEY CAN LEARN
THROUGH PRACTICE, **E**XPERIMENTATION AND MORE PRACTICE

PARENTS **F**EEL CONFIDENT AND DON'T COMPARE
THEIR CHILDREN WITH OTHERS

THEY WEAR **G**LASSES IF THEY NEED THEM

BOOKS ARE PART OF A FAMILY **H**OLIDAY

THE ARE ALLOWED TO READ WHATEVER
INTERESTS THEM AT THE TIME

THEY ARE NOT RIDICULED OR **J**UDGED FOR
THEIR INTEREST IN BOOKS

THEY **K**NOW HOW TO SPEAK CLEARLY WHEN
THEY READ OUT LOUD

THEY GET PLENTY OF CHANCES TO READ OUT **L**OUD EVEN IF
THEY CAN READ VERY FLUENTLY

WHEN THEY LISTEN TO READING THEY **M**AKE SURE
TO SIT WHERE THEY CAN HEAR

THEY MAKE THEIR OWN SCRAPBOOKS, SIGNS,
LABELS AND **N**OTICES

THEY GET PLENTY OF **O**PPORTUNITIES TO BROWSE EITHER IN A
BOOK SHOP OR A LIBRARY

They see other people, family and friends,
reading for **P**leasure and information

They are not re**Q**uired to read the books their
parents enjoyed as children

They see there is **R**eading everywhere — signs,
backs of packets, gates and doors

They go at their own pace and their
parents are **S**upportive

Their parents have **T**ime to share the fun
of books with them

They read in all the languages they **U**se

They hear other people reading aloud: parents, teachers,
storytellers on **TV**, the radio or at the library

They get the chance to '**W**rite' for other
people to read

They are not e**X**pected to be able to read things first go

Their parents have a sensible **Y**ardstick, keep their
sense of humour and common sense when they
hear what experts have to say!

Their reading skills give parents a bu**Z**z!

Reading is a life long pleasure and the more you do the more you get out of it. So, you are right to be interested in your child's reading.

ADULTS WHO CAN READ FEEL:

♦ part of society
♦ confident
♦ happy to help their own children
♦ willing to join in anything where they might have to read
♦ that their job opportunities are unlimited
♦ that further education is possible
♦ that forms are manageable
♦ that they can learn

CHILDREN WHO CAN READ HAVE:

♦ the delight of discovering things in books
♦ the chance to use computers properly
♦ the fun of sharing books
♦ the enjoyment of being able to 'disappear with a book'
♦ the ability to find information for themselves

Parents have become muddled by the methods used to teach reading over the years. The media announce a revolutionary new method which will solve all the country's reading problems, parents, teachers and education officials jump on the bandwagon! The ideas themselves have often been useful and have helped many kids get started, but none has ever been a universal miracle cure. So don't panic if one or more approved system doesn't work for your child.

HERE'S HOW WE TEACH KIDS TO READ.

CREATING A BOOKWORM

Don't do it *to* your child, do it *with* your child!

Set your goals together – you both want your child to be able to read so that your child:

- will love books, feel confident and competent in any situation where reading is required
- will be able to read anything
- will be sensitive to other kids when they're reading
- is confident about reading out loud
- is happy about reading things two or three times in order to be able to understand them
- recognises that new insights can be gained in each reading of a piece of writing where the ideas are complex
- will not be frightened of complexity or simplicity
- feels that learning is possible from anything
- understands people will want to read different things
- is happy to use a dictionary thesaurus, and encyclopedia to explore and to discover more about a subject

Once you have both agreed, get ready to start but . . . go slow to go fast!

Remember, learning to read is like moving into a new house. Some of the furniture can go straight into some of the rooms. Other rooms will need decorating before you can put anything in them. You will also want to go and look for special items that will go with your new home. With reading, children have some skills they can make use of, while other skills they will need to acquire from scratch and some skills they can learn when needed. Furnishing your home is a matter of personal preference, and so is learning to read!

Because learning styles are very different, it is essential to realise that there are many ways a child learns to read. If you provide your child with different routes you will be able to see which ones suit. Don't be anxious about routes your child doesn't like – there will be others he or she does.

ROUTES TO SUCCESSFUL READING

– through writing

Tim was five and had shown no interest in reading or writing until one day he became absorbed in a toy which, when he turned it over, had bubbles in it. Tim began to use words to describe what the toy was doing at a vocabulary level above anything any of us had heard him use before. He wanted to have a conversation about what was happening and enjoyed hearing other people's words which described what they could see. He was excited and wanted a record of what he had been doing. He managed to draw circles for the bubbles and colour them in. That was the beginning of Tim learning to draw letters which had circles.

For a long time Tim could only identify letters when he wrote them. Gradually he became more confident about reading letters wherever they were. Until he could write his own letters he was not interested in learning to read.

– through conversation

Talk to your child. The more we talk to children, the more they will understand how language works and the easier they will find it to understand what they are reading. When children discover that what they read can be the same as what they say, their reading will take off.

– through labelling

Labels are found everywhere. When you are out, your child can gradually learn lots of words that will be seen again and again, such as 'Bus Stop', 'For Sale', 'Safeway', 'push', 'pull,' 'open', 'closed'.

At home you can make labels for each room in the house and for belongings, 'Natasha's pencil case'.

A good labelling game is to have different verbs like 'go', 'come', 'skip' and 'sit', written on separate pieces of paper. The child's name is on a piece of paper. When you hold up a name and a verb the child has to do what it says, 'Karina skip'. This is a 'whole word' approach.

– *through sounds*

Lizzie was seven and had not made any progress in reading. She couldn't do a 'whole word' approach. When she finally learned all her letter sounds she suddenly understood that there was a way to read whole words. By using the sounds for 'c', 'a' and 't' and putting them together she realised she had 'cat'.

It took Lizzie many months to learn sight words (that is, words where the letters can't be used to sound them out when reading or spelling), such as 'they', 'there' and 'who'. However, during this time she was building up her reading of longer words like 'cannot', as long as she could sound them.

– *through desire*

A child can want to read so much that he asks for clues when he is reading. You can tell if your child has this approach from a question like, 'What does that word say, Mum?'.

– *through discovery*

Children learning through discovery will notice similarities between words. If they know one word they will look for that word everywhere. They may make lists of words that are similar, those that have the same number of letters and so on. Remember, learning happens for your child when you are learning at the same time as your child. You will be learning how to help through observing how your child learns, what excites your child, what keeps your child going, and what makes your child want to give up.

MAKING READING MORE MANAGEABLE

Let's look at this typical page from a reading book.

> Jennifer sat at the window, looking at the rain. She
> could hear the sound of her mother and Andy her brother,
> arguing as usual in the kitchen. Mum wanted them both to go
> with her to the hospital to visit Mr. Brown from next door. He
> had broken his leg when he fell over Jennifer's bike. Jennifer
> felt sick when she thought about the accident and wished she
> had put her bike away properly in the garage. Mum was
> always telling them to tidy up and from now
> on, Jennifer thought, she wasn't going to leave
> anything in the wrong place.

This page can be made manageable through identifying:

♦ sentences: how many are there?

♦ names: what are the different names on the page and how often do they appear?

♦ words that have at least two letters in the same sequence.

On this page the list would include:

s_at_	wi_n_dow	argu_ing_	go_ing_
_at_	look_ing_	tell_ing_	anyth_ing_

♦ words that have the same number of letters: make lists

2	3	—4	5 —	6—	7	8
in	now	tidy	going	mother	thought	properly
at	the	hear	usual	wished	arguing	anything

♦ word strings, when two words the same follow each other

at the window	_at the_ rain	
in the kitchen	_in the_ garage	_in the_ wrong place

- ◆ words that don't sound the way they are spelt

could	sound	thought	wanted
door	garage	accident	hear

- ◆ words which end in 'y'

properly   tidy

- ◆ words which end in 'ing' and 'ed'

looking	arguing	wished	telling
going	anything	wanted	

- ◆ words which have two vowels together

could	rain	sound	arguing
usual	thought	leave	

Discuss briefly whether the two vowels are sounded (e.g. the 'ua' in 'usual') or one of the vowels is silent (e.g. the 'i' in 'rain'), or whether the two vowels together make a different sound than either of them apart (e.g. the 'ou' in thought).

- ◆ words which have a 'u' and/or a 'c' in them

could   sound   accident   arguing   usual sick

These words are often difficult to read so it is useful to have identified them first.

- ◆ nouns: naming words

Jennifer	window	rain	bike
garage	mum	accident	hospital

- ◆ verbs: doing words

sat   fell   pushed   wished

- ◆ adjectives: describing words

wrong

- ◆ silent letters

'w' in wrong   'i' in rain

- ◆ words your child claims still not to know how to read even after the discussion.

Doing any or all of the above will make the page manageable because it is broken down into many parts (deconstruction). Your child will feel empowered by now making sentences using some of the words and reading the sentences to you (reconstruction).

SUPPORTING A CHILD
FROM COCOON TO FLIGHT

Children who know they will have support when they need it will become adventurous. Children who are ignored or forced to run before they can walk, especially with no support, will become timid, aggressive or try to be invisible.

You can support your child best by giving close support when it is needed. 'Close support' means you and your child focus on the same part of the activity at the same time. For example, if you are making a page manageable you might both be writing down words. If your child is writing a list you will be watching and supporting.

Your support may take the form of showing your child how the effort can be more rewarding, or congratulating your child on the advances being made. The reason for giving close support is to provide a cocoon in which your child can grow to the next stage where it is time to be slightly more independent.

Giving close support when reading

- Sit physically close so you can see what your child can see. Your child may be on your knee, next to you on the couch, or by you at the table.

- Listen very carefully to everything your child is reading and try to understand the logic of any mistakes. Your child may have guessed at a word after looking at a picture, may have confused a letter shape, or may not know a particular combination of letters (e.g. 'or' in corn; 'ght' in right).

- Have a pencil and paper alongside so whenever there is a mistake you stop and show your child how the word is broken down (e.g. 'that' is 'th' and 'at'.

- Remember to say how well your child is doing.

- Ask what your child thinks has been learned and say what you think has been learned — write it down.

- Use a relaxation if your child is losing his confidence or if it seems sensible as a break. See Appendix.

Spelling
and
Writing

COMPLEX SENTENCES

To keep soaring, children need to be encouraged to keep adding to their repertoired of reading skills and not become complacent.

To take full advantage of reading in order to reach their academic potential, children need to be able to handle a complex sentence about a simple subject.

The cat sat on the mat.

The cat was sitting on the mat.

The grey, fluffy cat was sitting on the mat.

The grey, fluffy cat was lounging on the carpet.

On the Persian carpet lounged a Himalayan cat.

Wooster, the Himalayan mouse catcher, lounged languidly on the expensive Persian carpet.

The supercilious Himalayan mouse catcher, known to his doting human family as Wooster, lounged languidly on the rare and expensive Persian carpet; dreaming of his foray into the shopping bag from which he had purloined the langoustines.

How to handle complex sentences – in newspapers and magazines

Find something that your child is interested in reading about then get your child to find an article on that subject in the paper.

Begin 'reading a sentence about', which means taking it in turn to read a sentence.

If there is something your child doesn't understand, look at the ideas in *How to handle complex sentences in schoolbooks.*

Newspapers are important because they give you immediate information which you can go back to, unlike television or radio. Newspapers will increase your child's knowledge of the world and local community, and of individuals within that world and community. They will give your child experience of many different forms of writing. Newspapers are the place where the newest words – which may become everyday words – appear.

How to handle complex sentences in story books

A storybook will:

♦ involve you
♦ have you thinking
♦ force you to draw on your powers of empathy
♦ lead you to empathise with people quite different from yourself
♦ provide you with language which will develop your thinking

The best way to read storybooks with your child is to read together. Explore the words and ideas as you go. Don't feel you have to read the whole book in this way. Your child may choose to keep reading at his or her own pace. Time set aside for reading aloud with each other is time well spent. Even when your child gets to secondary school, reading aloud helps develop understanding and enthusiasm.

How to handle complex sentences in schoolbooks

Children need to know specialist terms and their definitions when using a schoolbook. Sometimes a book will use a common word. Children may think they know what it means and then find they don't.

The Roman centurion carried a torch.

The agreement between the nations was cemented in Washington.

There were many privates at this time in the army.

Linus Pauling was a famous chemist.

Often children get caught out by two people having the same name. It can come as a surprise to discover there have been two Madonnas. Equally, Nelson Mandela is often assumed to have won the Battle of Trafalgar!

If a sentence in a schoolbook is in italics or bold print, it often means the definition for the word is in a glossary at the back. If not, the index can lead the reader to find the definition by looking at the first place the word has been mentioned.

'Reading a sentence about' with you can be another way of shedding light on the information. You might find it helpful to read the sentence over a few times, changing the emphasis on certain words, to grasp the meaning.

Together you could write down your own meanings for each word. This will help your child to see there are often several definitions for the same term.

Remember, a text book has been written to carry information from the writer to the reader. It is not the only place that the information can be found, it is one of the places.

Even adults can find the picture book on the subject an easier place to start, and work up from there.

How to handle complex sentences

Punctuation: stop, start and go!
If your child cannot make sense of a difficult sentence, look at the punctuation first. By pausing at a comma, semi-colon or colon, the meaning of the sentence can often become clear.

Searching for the missing word: dictionaries and encyclopaedias
If we check a word we are unsure of in the dictionary, it may give us a definition that helps us make sense of a sentence. Encyclopaedias may give a fuller description of the word.

What's it really saying?: the context
What is the context for the sentence? What was the sentence before about? Does that help you work out what comes next?

By turning the words into pictures
Where a word picture is created, ask your child to draw a picture of it on a piece of paper. 'There were 13 houses down that street, six on one side and seven on the other. The empty space was a playground.'

By turning the words into actions
If an activity or a posture is being described, get your child to act it out. 'He sat with his head in his hands, looking forlorn.'

By having a chat
Explore sentences that don't lend themselves to acting or drawing by discussing what they might mean or what it's like to feel that way.

skills that help with reading from the start

♦ holding the book the right way up

♦ turning the pages carefully

♦ looking at the pictures and listening to the story

♦ knowing the front of the book from the back

♦ going from left to right

♦ going from top to bottom

♦ knowing where the story comes from – that the squiggles are what Daddy is reading

♦ knowing what to choose

♦ thinking books are fun

♦ knowing that a book is ideas written down

skills that help maintain reading

♦ knowing the letter sounds and names

♦ knowing the alphabet (See *How to teach the alphabet* in Chapter 5)

♦ knowing how to put the letter sounds together to make a word

♦ knowing words do not always say what you would expect

♦ knowing the writing makes sense

♦ knowing how to find the books yourself

♦ knowing how to structure sentences so people understand your ideas

♦ see *The A – Z of successful reading* at the beginning of this chapter

Skills that make bookworms glow

♦ knowing how to get information out of a book

♦ being able to use an index, contents and glossary

♦ choosing what is helpful from what is unhelpful

♦ knowing how to read illustrations, graphs and tables of data

♦ thinking of questions that will help you to find the information you need

♦ remembering what you like so you will be able to get it next time

♦ recognising authors have particular styles

♦ knowing you have the skills to be able to work out what has been written, even if it takes a little time

♦ knowing why you like books

OVERCOMING COMMON PROBLEMS

THE BOY WHO JUST WOULDN'T TRY

David was 11 and just starting secondary school. His reading was alarming and irritating because he couldn't even get the two-letter words right. David felt that there was just no point in trying.

There are some things to do to help your child if you know your child can read some words but just won't.

1. Get him to look at the first sentence and write down any words he knows he can't read.

2. Help him to work out how to read them – break them up, look for two letters together that make a sound.

3. Now get him to read the whole sentence.

4. He can use the same method on the second sentence.

5. Get him to re-read the first and second sentences and then carry on to the next two sentences.

6. As soon as he stops trying, get him to look at the sentence like he did with the first one.

THE BOY WHO THOUGHT
HE COULD LEARN TO
READ IN A MINUTE

John was seven and the best footballer in the class, but he couldn't read.
He found this hard to understand because he shone in everything else.
He would begin every reading lesson feeling optimistic but as soon as he
made a mistake he would be furious with himself.

Here are some things to do if you know your child is losing confidence.

1. Decide together what you're going to work on – it could be reading all the two-letter words and then finding a sentence that has at least one of those words.
2. Your child could choose a word that is repeated in the book, such as the name of a character, and find sentences which contain that word.
3. Then your child finds the two-letter words in the sentence and reads them.
4. Now your child can have a go at reading the whole sentence.

You will feel exhausted by this little person who is being so hard on himself, but remember that you are the parent and you know he will succeed.

THE GIRL WHO MADE
SILLY MISTAKES

Alex was a confident and fluent reader but nothing she read made sense
because she left out letters or words. She thought she was a good reader
because her teachers didn't stop her and she got through lots of pages and
was on the hardest book in her class.

How you can help your child if they read carelessly.

1. You need to develop your child's ability to see all the bits of the sentence and get her to understand that what she is reading should make sense.
2. Get your child to read to you but as soon as she makes a mistake, she has to start again. This is an enjoyable game as your child keeps trying to get further each time.

This is an example of quality being preferable to quantity!

THE BOY WHO WAS TOO SCARED TO READ

Adam would back away from a book as if it was a time bomb. He was so scared he wouldn't be able to do it. He mumbled and looked around in desperation.

Here's what to do if your child is scared of reading.

1. Try some of the suggestions in *Making reading more manageable* on page 110. That way the panic can be taken out and the excitement and challenge of reading put back in.

THE GIRL WHO HAD MET A GLASS CEILING

Sarah could read and read well but no one had noticed. She was a well behaved little girl who just accepted the reading books she was given. She could read these easily but accepted that her teacher must know best.

She was no longer learning to read and was in danger of never reaching her reading potential.

Here's what to do if your child has reached a 'glass ceiling'.

1. Just give her some more difficult reading matter. Notice any mistakes she is making and show her how to sort them out. Try some of the suggestions in *Making reading more manageable* on page 110.

CHAPTER 7

CREATING KIDS
WHO CAN WRITE

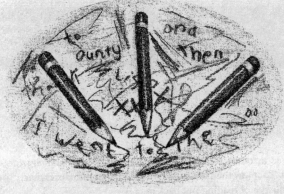

GETTING STARTED ON WRITING

WORDS, WORDS AND MORE WORDS

UNLOCKING IDEAS

POETRY

Through writing children have a direct line of communication to other people and are not dependent on anyone else. They can write letters to anyone, from the Prime Minister to the boy who moved away. They can write stories that are true or create whole worlds of their own. They can organise their lives with lists, labels and plans.

As children learn to write the letters of the alphabet they can begin to write their thoughts.

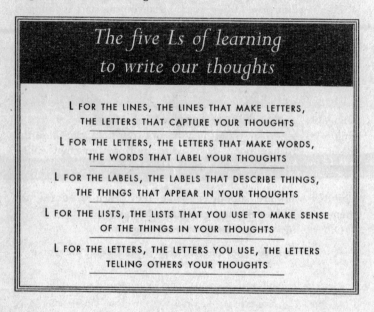

The five Ls of learning to write our thoughts

L FOR THE LINES, THE LINES THAT MAKE LETTERS, THE LETTERS THAT CAPTURE YOUR THOUGHTS

L FOR THE LETTERS, THE LETTERS THAT MAKE WORDS, THE WORDS THAT LABEL YOUR THOUGHTS

L FOR THE LABELS, THE LABELS THAT DESCRIBE THINGS, THE THINGS THAT APPEAR IN YOUR THOUGHTS

L FOR THE LISTS, THE LISTS THAT YOU USE TO MAKE SENSE OF THE THINGS IN YOUR THOUGHTS

L FOR THE LETTERS, THE LETTERS YOU USE, THE LETTERS TELLING OTHERS YOUR THOUGHTS

Dear Grandma,
Thank you for the book.

Look at the letter and think about what a writer would need to know to write it without help. In a group of parents, one wrote: 'A child would have to know how to use a pencil to make letters on paper. Next he would need to be able to put letters together to make words'.

One person wrote: 'The child would have to know what he was writing about, otherwise he might put the wrong words'.

Another wrote: 'He'd have to know how to spell or no-one would be able to understand it'.

Everyone agreed that if children knew that writing could be speech written down, they would have some idea of what they could write.

Then the parents began to wonder about how well the children would need to know any of these things in order to be able to write a simple letter.

They were surprised when we said that you can start as young as you like.

We explained that in just the same way that children are given books to play with well before they can read, children can become writers well before they can write!

Your child doesn't have to form all the letters alone, you can be a guiding hand. Take your child's hand in yours and if necessary help your child to hold the pencil as well as form the shapes. A child who can do an 'o', with or without your help, can fill in the 'o's in a word like 'book' if you write the rest. Your child will be excited at this mastery and burn to learn more.

Children who are supported while they learn to do it, for themselves, will see themselves as kids who can.

Other things you can do in this early stage are:

♦ write a whole sentence and your child writes over the top of your writing

♦ write the whole sentence and your child copies it

♦ write all the words that your child wants to put in the sentence in random order on a scrap of paper, then your child copies them down in sequence

♦ write the words and your child copies them into a word book which can then be used to make up sentences

Your child should always see the first attempt as a draft and not the finished product.

These are the technical skills that your child will need for writing. They will become more refined as your child progresses. The basic skills are forming letters, making words from the letters and making sentences from the words.

GETTING STARTED ON WRITING

How one word leads to another, then another and soon you've got a sentence

An excellent way for getting your child started on writing is to ask questions. Good words to include in questions are 'what', 'who', 'why', 'where', 'when' and 'how'.

You: **What** are you going to write?
Your child: A letter.

You: **Who** are you going to write to?
Your child: Grandma.

You: **Why** do you want to write to Grandma?
Your child: To thank her for my book.

You: Do you know **where** Grandma got it from?
Your child: No, but it was on my birthday list.

You: **When** did you look at the book?
Your child: Daddy read it to me last night.

You: **How** are you going to write the letter?
Your child: I'm going to say 'Dear Grandma, Thank you for the book'.

Extending conversations will mean that your child is in a good position for extending his or her writing as the act of writing gets easier. Your child will be able to use the technical skills which make sentences interesting and informative.

Writing good descriptions

Once your child can construct sentences, he or she will be ready to write stories. A good story writer sets the scene by adding description to the bare bones of the story.

A good way of getting started on a description is to take a

simple object such as an orange. Help your child to use their senses to describe the orange.

You: What can you **see**?
Your child: I can see an orange.

You: What does it **feel** like?
Your child: It feels soft and cold.

You: What does it **smell** like?
Your child: It smells tangy.

You: Does it make a **sound**?
Your child: Yes, when I tap it.

You: What do you think it would **taste** like?
Your child: Horrible, I hate oranges.

Now you can probe a bit more to get other ideas. Go back to some what, why, who, how, when questions.

You: What sort of orange is it?
Your child: It's a big navel orange.

You: Where did it come from?
Your child: We got it at the supermarket.

You: When did we get it?
Your child: Yesterday on the way home from school.

You: How can we use it?
Your child: I don't want to eat it but I could use it as a ball.

You: Who did we buy it for?
Your child: Grandma, because she likes them.

You: Why are we doing Grandma's shopping?
Your child: She's busy at work.

With all this information, your child could now think of a title for a story he or she could write about it the orange the title might be:

Our Shopping Trip

Grandma's Shopping

A Day In The Life Of An Orange

My Orange Ball

Questioning will get your child in the mood for thinking about the possibilities. Just as you can't expect your child to write words without letters, you can't expect him or her to write stories without descriptions.

When beginning to write stories using descriptions, your child may only manage one sentence, like:

'We went shopping'.

If you use the questions again, that sentence can be extended to:

Mummy and I went shopping yesterday
on our way home from school.

Or it could be: 'We went shopping at the supermarket yesterday and bought an orange for Grandma'.

Description doesn't only have to be about objects. Some story titles lend themselves to writing about feelings.

Why write that?

Children can be helped to understand why they are writing if they look at the first sentence of a book, an article or a comic, then think of all the questions they want to ask.

'I'M GOING TO TELL THE HEADMASTER,' SHE SAID.

1. What's she going to tell him?
2. Who is she talking to?
3. What has happened?

4. Why does she think the Headmaster will be interested?

5. What does she want the Headmaster to do?

6. What sort of school is she at?

7. Who is she?

8. How old is she?

Or they might even use a sentence which seems to be pretty ordinary.

IT WAS RAINING.

1. Does it matter that it was raining?

2. Is there anybody there?

3. Where are they?

4. Which country?

5. Is the sentence about a town?

6. Has it been raining long?

7. Which season is it?

8. Is the rain going to stop?

9. Which year is the story about?

This technique works well when you are reading. Read the opening sentence: what questions do you want to ask? Read on and see if those questions are answered as you read.

Writing is boring. I hate it.

When your child can't think of anything to write, try to keep the door open. Don't go at it head on. Have a conversation and write it down.

You: Tell me how you feel.

Your child: It's boring.

You: What's boring?

Your child: Writing stories is boring.

You: Who thinks writing stories is boring?

Your child: I think writing stories is boring.

You: Why is it boring?

Your child: I can't do it.

You:	Well, let me help you. What is less boring than writing stories?
Your child:	Watching TV is less boring than writing stories because I can change channels.
You:	Tell me why you like your favourite program. Now let's see if we can think of any sentence that might go in a story about this TV program.

A feeling for writing

Children have deep feelings which they can have difficulty expressing. This is partly because children don't know the words that explain the way they feel. It could also be because they aren't given the time or the space to explore the whys and wherefores of their world. Sometimes the time and space is available but the child is preoccupied with something else.

For example, a friend fell off a ladder and her two children who were six and seven thought it was the funniest thing they had ever seen their mother do. She pleaded with them to get someone to help but it was many minutes before they could stop laughing and really start listening. These weren't aberrant children. In another situation the same children would be kind, caring and very helpful to their mother, particularly if she had a headache.

This inability to be consistent about appropriate feelings doesn't disappear as one gets older. However, feeling words are an asset to everybody because they enrich communication.

An interesting game to play is to collect feeling words, one for each letter of the alphabet. This gives you lots of opportunities to talk about different feelings.

The A-Z of feeling words

Angry	Naughty
Bad-tempered	Obnoxious
Cross	Proud
Delighted	Quiet
Energetic	Rotten
Fidgety	Sad
Grumpy	Timid
Happy	Uncomfortable
Indifferent	Vexed
Jealous	Washed out
Kind	eXcited
Loving	Yucky
Miserable	Zappy

Now you can try using these words in sentences.

> I was cross when we went shopping.

> Yesterday I was excited because we bought an orange for Grandma at the supermarket.

> I felt angry and bad-tempered when Mum said we had to go to the supermarket until I realised we were buying oranges for Grandma.

By enlarging your child's vocabulary, you will enable your child to describe events and feelings more precisely. Your child will be a writer who is not limited to a few phrases.

Sometimes children get stuck with using 'like', 'hate', 'nice', 'good' and 'boring' to explain everything. Dinner was nice, her jumper is nice, her favourite television program is nice, her birthday party was nice, the two-week trip to Disney World was nice, her hamster is nice and so is her baby sister!

Expanding vocabulary helps a child to move past this stage.

WORDS, WORDS AND MORE WORDS

One effective way of getting your child to use a variety of words is to use a thesaurus.

1. Take a sentence like 'Dinner was nice.'

   At this point, if you're using an adult thesaurus, don't try looking up 'nice' because lots of the alternative words listed for 'nice' will not be appropriate for the sentence your child is writing.

2. Get your child to think of any words he or she already knows which could replace 'nice' in the sentence.

   Dinner was tasty.

   Dinner was delicious.

3. Now ask your child to look up 'tasty' and 'delicious' in a thesaurus to find other words that could be used to describe dinner:

   Dinner was flavourful.

   Dinner was appetising.

   Dinner was luscious.

   Dinner was delightful.

4. The activity could stop there but it is worth going on and looking up one of the new words to find even more alternatives. By looking up appetising, for example, you might find 'appealing' and 'inviting', 'tempting' and 'tantalising'.

5. Don't just stop with the synonyms (words that mean the same). Your thesaurus may also give antonyms (words that mean the opposite). As well as finding alternative and improved ways of saying 'Dinner was nice', your child will also discover a host of alternatives for 'Dinner was not nice'.

   Dinner was unappetising.

   Dinner was repugnant.

   Dinner was revolting.

   Dinner was terrible.

   Dinner was tasteless.

Rolling along

A rolling story can be a lovely way to get children expanding their ability to write. If your child sits in front of a blank page looking puzzled, or bounces in wanting to write but goes off the point, start with a sentence. This can be a sentence suggested by the homework or just any topic you or your child feel like using. You add the next sentence, and your child adds the next. The story just rolls along ...

THE THANK YOU LETTER

Dear Aunty Anne (HERS),

Thank you for the present (YOURS). I like my jumper very much (HERS). The colour is my favourite (YOURS). I wore it on Sunday (HERS). Mum says I look gorgeous (YOURS).

Lots of love

NEWS

I went to the beach (HIS). It was a bit cold (YOURS). I went swimming (HIS). My brother was trying out his surfboard (YOURS). I wish I could swim like him but I can't (HIS). Afterwards we went to my best friends to play (YOURS). We had a barbecue and then we had a swim in his pool (HIS).

All the words with...

Another exercise which children love is thinking of all the words which have two letters somewhere in them, such as all the words with 'bl'.

blood blame black blade blunt blue blot
blip blunder bladder blink blind

From these your child can make sentences.

I had blood on my hand after I cut it with the blunt blade.

The words can be used for tongue twisters.

The black blot blundered on the blue blotter and I blinked.

Your child could also make a list where the two letters can be found anywhere in the word.

able   terri**ble**   sensi**ble**   a**bl**ution   wob**ble**   rum**ble**

What happened before and what happened after

A DAY IN THE LIFE OF A DOLLAR

> The dollar was on the ground.

Where was it before it was on the ground?

> The dollar was in the little boy's hand and he dropped it.

What happened to the little boy?

> The little boy realised he lost it and he cried.

What happened to the dollar?

> The dollar lay there and it began to rain.

What happened next?

> A man came by and picked it up.

Where had this man come from?

> A man on his way home from work picked up the dollar.

Where did he put it?

> He put the dollar in his pocket and the dollar felt safe.

At some point your child will probably want to continue the story on his own. If not, keep helping until you get to the end.

ON AND ON AND ON – a 'sentencethon'

This is an exercise in how to turn a short sentence into a long sentence using conjunctions such as 'when', 'until', 'before', 'and', 'but,' 'however', 'yet', 'unless', 'therefore' and 'because'.

Ask your child to write a sentence.

I went shopping.

Now see if your child can use the word 'because' at the end of the sentence.

I went shopping because I had to get my uniform.

Now see if your child can use another conjunction.

I went shopping because I had to get my
uniform before starting back at school.

And another one?

I went shopping because I had to get my
uniform before starting back to school,
however there were no blazers in my size.

UNLOCKING IDEAS

Interviewing

This is a great technique for getting into a topic or helping unlock ideas in a child who thinks writing is difficult.

This means as well as the usual questions – 'who? what? when? where? why? how?', you can add questions that begin 'Do you ...? Are you ...? Can you ...? Will you ...? Have you ...? Would you ...? Could you ...?'.

What to do if your child comes home from school looking fed up and saying she has to write a page about Life in Roman Times!

Together draw up a list of interview questions that could be put to a Roman citizen.

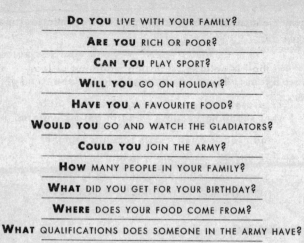

Do you live with your family?

Are you rich or poor?

Can you play sport?

Will you go on holiday?

Have you a favourite food?

Would you go and watch the gladiators?

Could you join the army?

How many people in your family?

What did you get for your birthday?

Where does your food come from?

What qualifications does someone in the army have?

Just by answering these questions with a bit of imagination you would have a good page of homework. If your child is interested in exploring life in Roman times, you can use the dictionary, encyclopaedia or specialist books.

Making links

With your child, choose six items (or more) to put on a tray. Now describe each item in as much detail as you can.

What does it look like?

What is it for?

What colour is it?

Let's say the items are a ball, eraser, paper clip, comic, toy car and orange peel.

The ball is yellow, small and made out of foam.
I use it to flick at people.

The eraser used to be white but is now grubby.

The paper clip is red, made out of plastic
and used to keep mum's receipts together.

It's my comic and I like it because
it is full of adventures.

The toy car is blue and it is old-fashioned
and I use it to play with.

I found the orange peel under my bed –
its orangey but it is drying out.

Now see if you can make links.

Mum bought a toy car for me at the shop on the same
day as I bought a comic. She put the receipt in the paper
clip with the others. When she put the receipts in the
drawer she found my eraser and put it in my bedroom
where I was flicking my yellow ball. It went on the
floor and she bent down to pick it up and saw...

A story from boxes

Choose a fairly simple object for the story, such as a hat. Now list all the sorts of hats, who wears a hat, why people wear hats and what a hat might be made of.

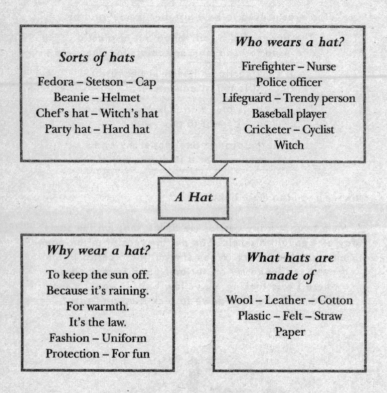

Sorts of hats

Fedora – Stetson – Cap
Beanie – Helmet
Chef's hat – Witch's hat
Party hat – Hard hat

Who wears a hat?

Firefighter – Nurse
Police officer
Lifeguard – Trendy person
Baseball player
Cricketer – Cyclist
Witch

A Hat

Why wear a hat?

To keep the sun off.
Because it's raining.
For warmth.
It's the law.
Fashion – Uniform
Protection – For fun

What hats are made of

Wool – Leather – Cotton
Plastic – Felt – Straw
Paper

Choose one word out of each box and see if your child can weave them into a story. By having had the time to think about the subject, jot down some words and organise them, your child may be well on the way to an idea of a story.

POETRY

Your child comes home from school demanding that you help write a poem about summer. You are horrified because you hated poetry at school. Don't panic! Here are four easy ways to write a poem.

Senses

YOUR QUESTIONS	YOUR CHILD'S POEM
Imagine a summer day. What can you see?	I can see children playing in the playground
What can you smell?	I can smell barbecues
What can you hear?	Dogs barking
What can you feel, touch?	The new beach towel
What can you taste?	Fish and chips

With tiny adjustments, you have a poem about summer.

First letters

Alternatively you could try an acrostic verse.

Write the letters of 'Summer Day' down the left hand side of a piece of paper. Now your child has to think of a line beginning with each letter.

Sunshine drying up the grass.

Umbrellas offering shade.

Mango ripe in the bowl.

Me getting hot at school.

Everyone gathering

Round the pool after work.

Dusty gardens,

Arid deserts,

Yellow, melting sun.

This Is

Poems don't have to be about great love or great beauty. They can be about things as ordinary as the kitchen!

> This is the fridge that keeps the food fresh.
>
> This is the bag that hangs on the door.
>
> This is the drawer for the knives and forks.
>
> This is the light switch for use in the dark.
>
> This is the sink where I have to wash up.
>
> This is the cupboard where the biscuits are hidden.

Whenever your child is writing a poem, get him or her to say it out loud to hear the rhythm and the flow that the words are making.

Repeat After Me

Using a little chorus can bring odd thoughts together to make a poem.

> The clock is ticking,
>
> Tick tock, tick tock.
>
> The kettle boils,
>
> Tick tock, tick tock.
>
> Mum comes in,
>
> Tick tock, tick tock.
>
> The television is on,
>
> Tick tock, tick tock.
>
> The tea is poured.

CHAPTER 8

CREATING KIDS WHO CAN DO MATHS

THE LANGUAGE OF MATHS

STARTING TO COUNT

WHEN YOU RUN OUT OF FINGERS ...

THE 'HOW TO' OF MATHS

FIVE LOTS OF 10 = 50 TIPS

Did you realise you are a good mathematician? Just think of the maths you've done today.

- ◆ Did you hop on the scales to check your weight when you got out of the shower?
- ◆ Did you hunt for some change for the bus fare?
- ◆ Did you compare prices in the supermarket?
- ◆ Did you get everyone out on time this morning?
- ◆ Did you check what you're going to watch on television tonight?

Well – it's all maths!

Every day we make calculations without even noticing. Maths is simply a way of writing down decisions about quantity.

- ◆ How much money is left in my purse?
- ◆ How many children can I fit in the car?
- ◆ There are more people coming for dinner than I have chops in the freezer.
- ◆ My salary is less than I need to live on – help!
- ◆ It's possible to use the carpet from my sister's to cover the hall.
- ◆ I must be fair to the kids and spend equal amounts on them at Christmas.

The A-Z of success in maths

Adding	Numbers
Borrowing	Ordering
Counting	Practising
Diagrams	Questioning
Equals	Reading
Figures	Symbols
Graphs	Tens
Hundreds	Units
Ideas	Volume
Jotting	Writing
Kilos	X=10 in Roman numerals
Listening	Years, months, days, hours
Multiplying	Zero is very important

THE LANGUAGE OF MATHS

Children can cope with maths questions when they know how to describe where something is.

It's <u>in front of</u> the television.

I'm sitting <u>next to</u> the window.

Our house is <u>between</u> two shops.

I put my toys <u>under</u> my bed.

I put the milk <u>in</u> the fridge.

Most maths questions deal with sequences. A sequence is an order in which one number follows another

Which number is in front of 7?
Which numbers come next to 16?
Which number is between 15 and 17?

Check if your child knows what the words in a maths question mean. A child who can explain what they mean is able to answer the question correctly. Children can describe what happens to quantities if they understand the meaning of the words 'and', 'make', 'share', 'more than', 'less than', 'difference' and 'take away'. Working with the digits that make up the numbers is easy once children understand these words.

Me _and_ my brother had 50 cents each and we put the money together to make a dollar. My brother took the money and bought some sweets. 50 + 50 = $1
My brother bought ten sweets and he shared them with me. 10 − 4 = 6; not 10 shared between two equally = 5
He got more than me and I got less than him. 6 > 4
Mum said we had different amounts. 6 − 4 = 2 but 5 − 5 = 0
My mum said it had to be fair shares so she took one from him and gave it to me. 6 − 1 = 4 + 1

Remember to use these simple words and make sure your child knows what they mean.

STARTING TO COUNT

When children are just learning to count, you can count anything and everything with them, from the number of socks in the wash to the number of birds feeding on the lawn. Each time you count things out loud they will be picking up the rhythm of counting: one... two... three... four... five... six.

Being able to count out things is important for understanding why so many numbers are necessary. Get your child to put all the spoons from the drawer out in a row and then count them. Your child should touch each spoon (or pick it up) while saying the numbers. This is known as 'one-to-one correspondence', which means linking the thing you are counting to a number.

Where's the maths in tidying up?

1. HOW PILES GET HIGHER AND GET LOWER

   Providing lots of opportunities to count as your child helps you tidy away toys, put away the washing or do the washing up means your child will gradually realise that when things are transferred from one place to another:

   ♦ one pile gets smaller while the other pile gets bigger
   ♦ you will get the same total if you count each item, one at a time, or if you put them into two piles, count each pile and then add them up
   ♦ each pile has a smaller number of items than there are all together

2. HOW LONG IT TAKES TO DO THE JOB

   Your child will learn how to tell the time if you provide lots of chances to see that the time you say actually relates to what is happening on a clock.

   Tell your child that you will tidy up for five minutes. Look at the clock and work out where the minute hand will be when you finish. Your child will become accustomed to how long five minutes is. 'I will be ready in five minutes' and 'The dinner will be on the table in ten minutes' help children understand time.

3. WHAT PILE SHOULD IT GO INTO?

   Your child can learn to categorise by colour, shape, size, or a group a toy belongs to. This helps with the understanding of maths because maths is about logic and patterns.

How to make five

Using the fingers on one hand, a child can learn how to put two numbers together to make a third number. By starting with the fingers on just one hand the child can use the other hand to help count or to hold down the fingers which are not being used.

Get your child to put one finger up and then another one. Then you can count: 'one and one make two'. Then continue, putting up three fingers and then another two to find out how five is made.

It is worth practising this sort of thing many times and one day your child will be able to tell you answers without using fingers.

Don't be impatient – getting the hang of this can take a long time. What your child will discover quickly is that his or her own hands can be used to do sums – a walking calculator!

What makes ten and why it's important

We live in a decimal system. When a child learns all the ways to make ten it will be easy to make hundreds, thousands and even millions. All children get excited the day they realise they have the power to add one million and one million and find the right answer!

Here are some ideas which might help you and your child describe what you are doing when you are explaining things to each other.

♦ Fingers are called digits in biology books. Numbers are called digits in maths books.

♦ The digits are 0, 1, 2, 3, 4, 5, 6, 7, 8 and 9 and they are used to form all the numbers.

♦ The digits are like letters, only they make numbers whereas letters make words. Each digit is one number (whereas only two letters are words on their own – 'a' and 'I').

♦ Zero cannot be counted on a finger because it doesn't describe anything you can touch – it only tells you there is nothing there. In fact it took a long time for our ancestors to realise that if they invented a digit for nothing they could do many things!

Ten can be said easily and, if a child understands how numbers are formed, when it comes to writing down 10 it will still be simple. Digits that have already been used – 0 and 1 – are put together to make a new number.

However, this can be a sticking point for children. To explain the number 10 you can use a story.

In the old days the only calculators people had were their fingers. If they needed to count more than 10 things and there was only one person to do the counting, he would count to 10 and then put down a stone or something else to keep a record of how many had been counted and then he would continue on his fingers until he had counted 10 again. He would put down another stone and keep going in the same way until he had finished counting everything he needed to. Each stone counted for ten. He would count up the pile of stones and count the number of fingers that he had up at the end of his counting. The number of tens he would write down on the left and the number of units he would write on the right.

One person's fingers equal 10 which is one 10 and no more. The 1 becomes 'one 10' and the 0 becomes 'no more': 10 = 1 ten and 0 more.

Sixty five would be 6 stones and 5 fingers or 65 = six tens and five more . . . but more of that later!

Zero is not for nothing

Be careful not to skip over explanations of what zero means. Because we tend to think of it as a nothing we can easily ignore what it's really there for. A zero in a number represents some value.

10 – here the zero tells us the one is worth 10

100 – here the zeros tell us that the one is worth 100

Some more information about nothing:

- ♦ When you add nothing to something there is no difference.
- ♦ When you take nothing away from something there is no difference.
- ♦ But when you multiply something by nothing you lose the lot!

When you run out of fingers ...

Your child first needs to be able to count to 10, then to be able to match the spoken word to a figure. Magnetic numbers on the fridge can help.

When this is mastered, you can teach your child to count to 20. Show your child how you use the same digits that were used to count to 10 to write the digits to 20.

Go at a sensible pace. If your child is getting numbers wrong, start again at a point where he or she understands and is getting them right. Encourage lots of practice.

Counting house

Tens and units is about exchanging. Your child needs to learn how 10 lots of one thing can become one lot of 10.

Take a pile of old one cent coins (or empty your child's money box!) and count how many cents there are in it. If there are more than 10, get your child to put them into piles of ten with the remaining cents being the last pile.

Let's say there are 43 cents, which will be four piles of 10 and three left over. Every time your child makes a pile with 10 cents in it, the pile can be exchanged for a 10 cent piece.

One way of doing this is to get your child to write out a number chart. This is good practice in counting up to a hundred.

Divide a piece of paper into a hundred squares, then number each square like this.

1	2	3	4	5	6	7	8	9	10
11	12	13	14	15	16	17	18	19	20
21	22	23	24	25	26	27	28	29	30
31	32	33	34	35	36	37	38	39	40
41	42	43	44	45	46	47	48	49	50
51	52	53	54	55	56	57	58	59	60
61	62	63	64	65	66	67	68	69	70
71	72	73	74	75	76	77	78	79	80
81	82	83	84	85	86	87	88	89	90
91	92	93	94	95	96	97	98	99	100

Get your child to put one cent in each space starting from 1, making sure not to miss any squares. Every time there is a whole row full, your child can take off the 10 one cent pieces and have one 10 cent piece.

Playing the exchange

Each child draws ten squares in a row and puts the numbers 1 to 10 in the squares.

1	2	3	4	5	6	7	8	9	10

Each child then draws another 10 squares with the numbers 10, 20 and so on up to 100.

10	20	30	40	50	60	70	80	90	100

The first player throws a dice and whatever number it lands on, the player takes that number of cents from the pile and puts them on his or her strip. The other players do the same.

When players reach more than 10 one cent pieces, they exchange 10 of them and instead puts a 10 cent piece on to the second strip.

Each player should explain what is happening during their turn.

> I'VE GOT FIVE AND NOW I'VE THROWN A SIX. FIVE AND SIX MAKE 11, WHICH IS ONE 10 (MAKES THE EXCHANGE) AND ONE LEFT OVER.

This game gives lots of practice in understanding the difficult ideas behind how a lot of things can be exchanged for just one thing that still has the same value.

Reading the numbers

You can explain the difference between 17 and 70 when your child can read the numbers up to 100. 17 is one ten and seven units, but 70 is seven tens and zero units. The fact that the 'teen' numbers and the 'ty' numbers sound so similar can cause confusion if you don't point out the difference.

Throwing numbers

Make two dice – one that goes up to six and one that has seven, eight, nine and three zeros.

You need the second dice so you can throw numbers where the digits are more than six or where they include zero.

Make a number chart 1 to 100.

The first player throws both dice. Let's say this gives six and eight.

The player decides whether it will be 68 or 86, and then crosses the chosen number off on the chart. The object is to see how many numbers can be covered up in a certain time. The player can choose to use one dice twice to fill in any gaps.

Using the number charts for higher and lower

This will help your child realise where numbers are in relation to each other.

You choose a number, but don't tell your child what you've chosen. Your child holds the number chart and suggests a number. Let's say you have chosen 11 and your child says 82. 11 is lower than 82, so you give the signal – point down with your thumb. Your child checks the chart and then says six. You give the signal that your child needs to think of a higher number now – the thumbs up. See how close your child can get in ten tries.

The number chart helps your child realise that numbers get bigger. When it comes to sums, your child will be better able to spot silly mistakes.

It may seem a little 'over the top' to be suggesting all these games, but as technology becomes more sophisticated children are missing out on lots of opportunities to practise numbers. When you go shopping you probably pay by plastic, when you book a theatre ticket you do it over the telephone and when you pay a gas bill you do it by standing order. This means that children don't hear numbers in everyday conversation in the same way we used to – hence the games!

The 'how to' of maths

Adding

The easiest sums to start with are the 'adds'. Before they can begin to work out sums which are written down, children need to learn:

- the add sign is a +
- the add sign means put the two numbers together by continuing to count
- the equal sign is =
- the equal sign means that the numbers on the left hand side can be put together to make the number on the right (5 + 3 = 8) and vice versa (8 = 3 + 5)
- they can do sums up to ten using their fingers

Give your child lots and lots of experience in sums which add up to 10 or less. Don't forget the 0!

1 + 3 =	2 + 2 =	6 + 4 =	1 + 1 =
4 + 4 =	3 + 1 =	5 + 5 =	2 + 0 =
4 + 6 =	4 + 0 =	7 + 3 =	0 + 2 =
1 + 1 =	0 + 4 =	2 + 8 =	3 + 3=

What happens to numbers which are bigger than ten?

Once a child realises there is a pattern, it is easy.
- If 5 and 4 make 9   then 15 and 4 make 19   and 115 and 4 make 119
- If 5 and 3 make 8   then 3 and 15 make 18   and 33 and 5 make 38
- If 5 and 5 make 10   then 5 and 15 make 20   and 115 and 5 make 120

Taking away

'Take aways' can be done on fingers too! Start by reminding your child what makes 10 and write it down.

5 + 5 = 10

Now get your child to show you on his or her fingers.

Then say 'Put five fingers down' and ask what has happened. Putting five fingers down is the same as taking five fingers away.

Then you could show how to write what has happened using the −
sign.

10 − 5

Ask what is left and that gives him the answer.

10 − 5 = 5

Remember to put the symbols into words so that your child knows they are not strange hieroglyphics but can be explained using words.

- ◆ Words for the + sign are 'plus', 'and', 'add on'.
- ◆ Words for the - sign are 'take away', 'minus', 'reduced by', 'less', 'subtract'.
- ◆ Words for the = sign are 'makes', 'equals', 'is the same as'.

Give lots of chances to practise.

It all adds up

Time spent on 'adds' and 'take aways' is time well spent because these skills form the basis of everything your child does in maths now and all through life. It may be hard to believe, when you look at your child's algebra much later, that 'a + b = 9 when a = 4 and b = 5' is still using the same idea as 4 + 5 = 9.

Multiplying

Multiplication is a quick way of adding the same number over and over again. You could do 9 + 9 + 9 + 9 + 9 and find out that it equals 45, or you could say 9 x 5 = 45. Same answer, but one way is quicker!

- ◆ Words for the x sign are 'multiply', 'times', 'lots of', 'sets of'.

To teach multiplication, get out the cents again. Give your child a handful of one cent pieces and get him or her to count out ten. Then ask your child to put them out in piles of two. Ask what you've got now. Don't be discouraged if the answer isn't exactly what you had in mind. What you want is for your child to see what is happening, so keep asking questions which will help him or her understand what has been done. If your child gets confused, go back to the starting point.

You:	What did you start with?
Your child:	A pile.
You:	What was in the pile?
Your child:	Ten cents. (Writes the number 10)
You:	What did you do with them?
Your child:	I put them out.
You:	How did you put them out?
Your child:	In piles.
You:	How many were in each pile?
Your child:	Two. (Writes the number 2)
You:	How many piles have you got?
Your child:	Five. (Writes the number 5)
You:	So, can you tell me what's on the table?
Your child:	Five piles.
You:	Five piles of what?
Your child:	Five piles of two one-cent coins.
You:	Can you tell me how you write that? Do you know the sign for 'piles of'? What is that all together? (Writes 5 x 2 = 10)

Don't worry if your child cannot do this right away. At this stage what you're exploring is the idea of grouping. For multiplication, the groups are always equal – groups of two make the 2x, groups of three make the 3x, and groups of 100 make the 100x.

Now ask your child to put the 10 lots of one cent coins into piles of five. Your child may understand that 2 x 5 = 5 x 2, but don't worry if this has not happened yet. At least your child has seen that a pile can be made into groups. With guided experience and their own discoveries, your child will gradually understand.

Division

Any time you are doing this exercise, remind your child that division is part of multiplication. 'How many piles of two can you make from 10?' is the same as '10 divided by two'.

Another way to think of division is as repeated taking away. To find out how many twos there are in 10:

1. $10 - 2 = 8$
2. $8 - 2 = 6$
3. $6 - 2 = 4$
4. $4 - 2 = 2$
5. $2 - 2 = 0$

The answer is five. There are five lots of two in 10.

Remember, it may seem so simple to you but may be a total mystery to your child!

Children will become good at maths if they get practice. It really doesn't matter what they practise on – what you should be trying to do is give a lot of experience with what it is that makes a sum. Sums don't come out of thin air, they can always have a story behind them.

Children who understand there's a story and are even happy to make up their own will be comfortable with maths, undaunted by difficult sums and excited by new discoveries of how one thing relates to another.

Pictures can help

Get your child to draw a picture of what is happening. When learning the 2x, there are lots of ways. The tower one works rather well. The child draws two circles on the ground floor, and that shows that one lot of two makes two. Each time the child draws two more circles, he or she can see how the 2x happens.

5x	oo	= 10
4x	oo	= 8
3x	oo	= 6
2x	oo	= 4
1x	oo	= 2

Then the child can put the sums alongside. The child could draw pairs of boots, socks or gloves instead of just circles.

FIVE LOTS OF 10 = 50 TIPS

10 ways to make your child count

TEACH YOUR CHILD:

1. the odd and even numbers
2. words that describe position, such as 'next to', 'by', 'alongside', 'in between', 'before' and 'after'
3. how to draw a horizontal line and how to draw a vertical line
4. the shapes
5. how to use a ruler
6. that 60 seconds make a minute, 60 minutes make an hour, 24 hours make a day, 7 days make a week and 52 weeks make a year
7. the meaning of first, second, third, fourth, fifth and so on
8. that 100 cents make a dollar
9. how to describe a half and a quarter
10. the calendar – days of the week and months of the year

10 maths activities that count

1. Draw a bird's eye view plan of your child's bedroom.
2. Measure your child's handspan, height, arm stretch, head size, waist, leg length and shoe length.
3. Do a graph of the food in the cupboard.
4. Keep a chart of the weather.
5. Cut up apples into halves and quarters.
6. See how many cups of water it takes to fill a bowl and how many jugs of water it takes to fill the same bowl.
7. Have a play shop.
8. Keep a tally chart of words in your child's reading book.
9. Bake a cake!
10. Set the table!

10 things that make your home count

1. a height chart
2. a clock with a clear face that your child can look at and you can use together
3. scales
4. a ruler, scissors and glue
5. a tape measure
6. a piggy bank
7. a memo board – you could use it to write out timetables or people's birthdays or how many days until the holidays
8. jigsaws
9. a dice
10. building blocks

10 ways to made a trip to the shops count

1. Discuss whether there's going to be a lot of shopping or a little shopping and whether you'll need a bag.
2. Write a list together with the number of each item you'll need.
3. Decide which shops you are going to and plan the journey.
4. Tell your child how you're going to pay.
5. Check the weather and decide what's best to wear – might you need an umbrella?
6. Keep a note of how far away the shops are and time how long it takes to get there. On the way you could count the number of red cars.
7. When you're at the shops, involve your child – crossing things off the list, putting the fruit in a bag, taking the things off the shelves and telling you the prices.
8. When you get home your child can put things away in the right cupboards and fill up canisters.
9. Talk with your child afterwards about the trip – how many shops you went to, which things you bought which weren't on the list, and which things you forgot which were on the list!
10. While you have a well-deserved cup of tea, see if your child can remember what was bought. This activity helps your child to develop his or her memory. Perhaps with your child's help you won't forget anything next time!

10 more helpful hints which count

1. There are two types of ruler which your child needs to be able to use :

    ♦ one where you measure from the end of the ruler – this can be called a dead end ruler

    ♦ the other where you measure from the first mark – this can be called a waste end ruler

2. To use a ruler successfully, your child needs to know how to hold the ruler firmly in the middle so little fingers do not poke over the edge to give a bump in the beautiful straight line!

3. A sharp pencil will produce neat work. It's best to have a supply.

4. A right angle is made by joining a vertical line to a horizontal line.

5. There are four signs in maths to help calculate numbers. Usually + and x will give an answer bigger than the numbers you start with, while – and ÷ will give a smaller answer.

6. Your child will use tables all the time, not just for tables tests and multiplication sums, but for fractions, percentages, equations in algebra, statistics, matrices, probability, angles and area, perimeter and volume – in fact all through life. Knowing tables really well is a good start for success in maths.

7. You can do your 9x tables on your fingers. Put your fingers up so you can see the palms of your hands and count the thumb on the left as one and then all the other fingers from left to right until you get to the right thumb which will be 10. Then, if you want to know what 3 x 9 is, put the third finger down – the two fingers on the left will tell you how many tens and the seven fingers on the right will tell him how many units, so 3 x 9 = 27.

8. The maths your child learns before going to secondary school will be useful in Art, Physics, Chemistry, History – in fact it will pop up everywhere.

9. The maths you learned at school you are using now. Show your child how often you use it, so he or she can see that:

10. MATHS MATTERS.

CHAPTER 9

CREATING KIDS WHO CAN LEARN ... TO LIVE!

FOR STARTERS ...

GOOD TIMES AND BAD TIMES

KIDS WHO CAN, DO

Learning with your child can be fun when you accept that you are both only human.

Remember everyone feels good when feeling cared for, supported and liked.

The A-Z of self esteem

Appreciation	Needs
Back-up	Opportunity
Compassion	Praise
Dignity	Quality
Equality	Risk
Friends	Sympathy
Growth	Thoughtfulness
Harmony	Understanding
Interests	Vulnerability
Jubilation	eXchange
Kinship	Worth
Love	You
Motivation	Zing!

To get the best out of yourself and your child, you need to know what gets you both started, what keeps you going and what makes you feel fulfilled.

FOR STARTERS ...

How do you get started?

Some things you will do because it's too uncomfortable not to do them – you finally put out the compost bucket when it's overflowing or smelling disgusting!

Some things you will do because you feel you should – you offer to take 10 children to a football match because no-one else will!

Some things you will do because you enjoy them – you swim for a mile each morning because you love the exercise!

Some things you will do because you see a new opportunity – you take driving lessons so you can get a new job!

Some things you do because you have to – you miss part of a film because you have to answer the telephone!

Some things you will do because you can – you fill in a crossword puzzle because you are good at them!

Teaching a reluctant child to get started

Decide together how long the work should take, let's say 30 minutes to complete the worksheet. Set realistic goals, then check how much time is available. Let's say your child has two and a half hours before he or she goes to Scouts or Guides. Agree that in that time 30 minutes of work will be completed.

This will give your child experience in how to get started. Your child will get to know what it takes to get started when the spirit is unwilling and there is a time limit!

What keeps you going?

- ♦ a belief in yourself
- ♦ an interest in what is still to be done
- ♦ an understanding of what the whole task needs
- ♦ the right equipment
- ♦ enough information
- ♦ ability
- ♦ energy
- ♦ encouragement
- ♦ wanting to finish the job
- ♦ a picture in your mind of what it will be like when it is finished
- ♦ a memory of how hard work has paid off in the past
- ♦ knowing how to pace yourself

How to keep your child going

1. Your child can have a break but must have agreed the length of the break before it begins.

2. See how much your child can get done in two minutes — this changes the pace and can often be just as good as a rest.

3. Your child can tell you what has been finished so far.

4. Your child can read out loud what has been done so far.

5. Your child can tell you what he or she thinks still needs to be done.

6. Your child can have a stretch.

7. Your child can have a drink of water.

8. Your child can have a snack.

9. Rewriting what has been done can suddenly show your child where improvements could be made.

10. If your child has lost heart because the work is messy, rule a line and let him or her start again.

How to keep yourself going

When your child feels beaten and wants you to feel defeated too, both your batteries will be recharged by relaxation (see Appendix).

Keep in mind that this homework task may not be important in itself, but that keeping going when you want to give up is a skill for life. If you keep this in mind you won't get caught making excuses to yourself like 'my child's too tired' or 'I haven't got time'.

Check whether there is something your child really doesn't know which is causing the feeling of defeat and give as much support as your child *needs* to get started again – not wants, needs!

Listen carefully to what your child says is the problem. Sometimes it may be that your child is not able to concentrate because there is something else on his or her mind. Make sure you are not deflected, but let your child know that there will be a time to talk about it: 'We can talk about it now and do the work later, or do the work now and talk about it later'.

GOOD TIMES AND BAD TIMES

How to feel fulfilled

Feeling fulfilled comes when your dreams become reality and what you have planned takes shape. You can feel satisfied when you have used your skills to help another person make a discovery or improve techniques. You can feel fulfilled when you show someone you care, or when someone shows you that they appreciate you. You can get a lot of satisfaction from completing a task you found difficult. You can feel satisfied from a job well done.

How to give your child a sense of fulfilment

Get your child to set realistic goals. This doesn't mean you scoff at the idea of becoming Prime Minister, but encourage your child to see the steps that will be necessary to get to that goal.

Children who are optimistic about their ability to learn to set goals which allow them to experience a sense of fulfilment. This acts as a springboard for new learning.

How to feel fulfilled when working with your child

You and your child might both feel a sense of fulfilment, but for different reasons – your child might feel fulfilled because the homework is finished and you might feel fulfilled because it is set out better than your child has ever done before.

You will feel fulfilled if you have a list of areas where you want your child to improve and you notice improvements in any one of these areas.

The Mutual Appreciation Society

Both of you will respond best if you have the things you need from each other. Sometimes your child will make you feel better by smiling, paying attention to what you are saying and thanking you for your help.

Be sensitive to what your child needs from you – one day food may be welcome and the next day it is turned away. Remain calm and focused and remember what you are trying to achieve in the long run.

Children will always benefit from sincere praise. There are many things you can praise your child for so he or she will feel likeable even if some parts of your relationship have hit the rocks. If the homework has been done badly and you can't offer praise for it, make a conscious decision to note something you like about your child. This is not patronising, it just means a child knows that he or she is more than the homework to you.

If your child closes down on you

Children 'close down' at different times. They don't let their parents help even though the parents have offered. There are many reasons for this. Children can close down because they:

- ♦ feel you help too much
- ♦ feel you're not interested
- ♦ want to be an only child
- ♦ want to have brothers and sisters
- ♦ want a dog!
- ♦ are feeling guilty
- ♦ are lonely
- ♦ are embarrassed
- ♦ are impatient
- ♦ feel cross
- ♦ feel no good
- ♦ feel despair
- ♦ feel superior
- ♦ feel inferior

Don't despair, children do suffer but they can be helped to cope with the ups and downs of life. You may have to accept that your child loves you and knows that love is returned, but needs to ignore the support you are giving and refuse any additional support.

It's painful for sure! You can't win.

You are not alone.

If you are worried, enlist the support of someone your child knows, trusts and will listen to.

This person doesn't need to do any more than keep a watchful eye and listening ear out for your child. An opportunity may arise where your child might want to talk and this 'guardian angel' will be there to help.

Hectic times

There will be times in every child's life when he or she is not the most important person and you're so busy you just don't have time for everything you would like to do. This is normal – you don't need to feel guilty and your child doesn't need to feel aggrieved.

Perhaps a family member is very ill and you need to visit the hospital, look after the person's home and pay their bills. It could be you're doing a course which is proving very difficult, or maybe you've been promoted and have to put in long hours.

The best thing in a situation like this is to talk about the problem. Find out what will make both of you feel supported. You might need your child to take out the rubbish, your child might need a lift to the station. The needs themselves may not seem to be important, but they matter to you both as individuals so they are important. You might need to give your child a hug, and your child might need you to smile.

When someone interferes when you haven't asked for help

SOMEONE IS SURE YOU NEED HELP WORKING WITH YOUR CHILD

The father of a school friend of your son sees him being bullied at the bus stop and calls round to offer help.

If he offers to give your son a lift when he picks up his own son, to come with you to report it to the Headteacher, or to tell the other child off if he sees it happening again, you might be grateful for the help.

If he offers to go round and see the bully's parents on your behalf, tells your son to fight back or says he's organised his son and his mates to sort the bully out, you might wish he hadn't made any offers at all!

One way of coping with unwelcome help is to say what you are going to do. That way you turn yourself into a person who can rather than a person who can't.

YOUR PARTNER MAY KNOW SOMETHING YOU DON'T KNOW!

Your partner may have been sworn to secrecy and so can't tell you why your child is coming home late but is telling you not to worry. Your partner may know that your child has a paper round to earn money for a special present for you.

A FRIEND THINKS YOU ARE BEING UNFAIR

Adults can be unfair on children of the opposite sex simply because they haven't realised that what the child is doing is reasonable. They may need help from an adult of the child's sex to help point out what is reasonable from someone of that age and sex.

FAMILY AND FRIENDS CAN HELP YOU OR YOUR CHILD TO UNDERSTAND EACH OTHER'S FEELINGS IF YOUR EXPERIENCES ARE VERY DIFFERENT

Experiences can vary because of position in family:

- ◆ through birth: being an only child, the youngest child, a child in a large family, the oldest child, the only girl, the only boy
- ◆ through circumstance: being an adopted child, a fostered child, sent away to school, a child who doesn't know one parent

Experiences can vary because of trauma:

- ◆ being a child who has lost a brother or sister, a parent who's lost a child, a child who has a parent with mental health problems, a child who has a parent with chronic health problems, the child of a notorious parent, the child of someone who finds it very difficult to cope.

People might offer help if they can see that your child needs to hear an explanation for the way one of you is feeling and believes that you can't provide that explanation.

The rise of support groups is a result of people realising how a particular circumstance might be affecting them and wishing to share experiences with others who have been in the same position.

KIDS WHO CAN, DO

Kids who can are kids who know how to think and want to keep improving the way they think. They know how to recognise a problem and what to do when they come across one.

THEY USE THE FOLLOWING STEPS.

1. What do I know?
2. What do I need to know? What questions will I need to ask?
3. How will I plan?
4. Where will I find out?
5. How can I organise the information?
6. What have I learned?
7. How can I reorganise the information now?
8. What information is worth keeping for this problem and what will I set aside?
9. What new questions have arisen?

If they still don't have the answers, they repeat the steps.

How the method works for a school project

THE PROBLEM: TO COME UP WITH A NEW PLACE IN THE LOCAL AREA EVERY WEEK, AND TELL SOMEBODY HOW TO GET THERE.

1. What do I know?
   - the boundaries of my local area
   - places I've already visited and how to get to some of them by car
   - how to read a road map
   - where to get a bus timetable
   - some road names
   - how to draw a simple map

2. What do I need to know?

- ◆ what time the places open and close
- ◆ which months of the year the places are open
- ◆ if there are any entrance fees
- ◆ how to get to all the places by public transport or car
- ◆ any special events that are held at the places
- ◆ whether there is something there for all the family

3. How will I plan?

- ◆ organise what I've got so far – questions and answers into categories.
  - a) Places
  - b) Routes
  - c) Transport

4. Where can I find out?

- ◆ Places – tourist/information office, library, friends, local newspaper, guidebooks
- ◆ Routes – NRMA, personal visit
- ◆ Transport – bus depot, train station, phone

5. How can I organise the information?

A CHECKLIST OF WHAT I'VE COVERED

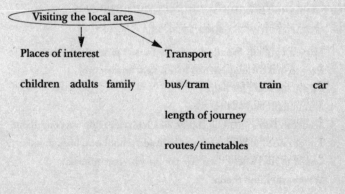

Visiting the local area

Places of interest

children   adults   family

Transport

bus/tram   train   car

length of journey

routes/timetables

Museum

- Interesting for whole family
- Special demonstrations – Monday, Thursday 2.00 pm
- Cafe – open 9.00 am - 4.00 pm
- Shop – open 9.00 am - 4.00 pm
- No entrance fee
- Seats in garden to eat lunch and relax
- Lots of hands-on activities for children
- Transport Route 30 from Central Railway stops outside museum – 10 minute journey. Walk 20 minutes. By car – plenty of cheap parking.

6. What have I learned?
   - how to read a bus timetable
   - where the places are and how to get there
   - what they offer

7. How can I reorganise the information now?
   - A separate piece of paper for each place in the folder.

8. What new questions have arisen?
   - Which are the best times and days to go?
   - Where are the best handouts available?

How the method works for personal problems

THE PROBLEM: HOW TO MAKE FRIENDS

1. I haven't got any friends. Everyone thinks I'm stupid. I like animals.
2. How to make friends? Why I haven't got any friends?
3. I'll ask my Mum for help.
4. Mum might know where to go.
5. What can I do something about? Which bit can't I do anything about?
6. I might need to look for friends outside school who like animals.
7. I need to find where there are people who like animals.
8. Where will I find them?

TURNING CAN'T DO INTO CAN DO THROUGH RELAXATION

WHY RELAXATION WORKS

HOW RELAXATION WORKS

Why relaxation works

Do you ever have days when you don't have a chance to sit down, let alone some time to think?

So do children!

KNOWING HOW TO RELAX IS A VALUABLE SKILL TO HAVE BECAUSE RELAXATION:

- ♦ takes the pressure off
- ♦ gives you a break
- ♦ makes it easier to remember things
- ♦ gets you back in touch with your body
- ♦ gives you energy
- ♦ makes it easier to plan
- ♦ makes it easier to like people
- ♦ makes you more likeable

FOR KIDS, RELAXATION MEANS:

- ♦ they learn faster
- ♦ they realise they are loved
- ♦ they become able to control how they feel
- ♦ they can enjoy other people
- ♦ they can make sense of the world
- ♦ they can use their imaginations
- ♦ they become more likeable people!

How relaxation works

It should be planned so it fits naturally into your working day. It will work best if there is a recognised time and place for it to happen.

If you are doing it with your child, explain before you start just what it involves. Check that what you're suggesting won't cause your child a problem.

The room you choose to relax in should be as quiet as possible. If necessary, unplug the telephone.

Relaxation can be done lying on the floor or sitting in a chair. The important thing is that there is plenty of space to stretch and make yourself comfortable.

There are probably as many ways to relax as there are ways of getting stressed. The following are very simple, require no training and are effective.

Take a deep breath!

In three seconds you can let go tension by taking a deep breath. If you can extend the time the benefits will increase. As you breathe, feel the air moving in through your nose. Notice the effect it is having on your body as you breathe in deeply. Control the out breath so that you establish a deep and rhythmical cycle which will be relaxing, calming and cleansing.

Use your eyes to harmonise

This is an ideal relaxation to use when you feel threatened. You simply notice the things around you.

I have two feet on the floor.
There are curtains at the window.
The lights are on.
There are daffodils in the vase.

As you notice things, you establish a rhythm to the sentences which has a calming effect on the mind.

One of the advantages of this relaxation is that it can be done with your eyes open, which means you can do it as you walk into an interview or a meeting with your child's teacher, you can do it in the supermarket queue or when you're waiting at the traffic lights.

Practise pausing

Decide you are going to make a definite break in what you are doing in order to go still. This helps you remember that you are in control of the task and not a robot being controlled by the task.

The break needs to be a few seconds during which you concentrate on one sense – it could be touch and you notice the feel of the tablecloth under your fingers.

Pausing is like going into neutral and giving the engine a break. When you carry on you will feel calmer, more focused and clear headed.

Going still

A 'going still' is a longer and more structured version of pausing. It creates a peaceful sense very quickly as you cut off from the stresses and strains around you. It calms the mind, gives you a break and helps you to restart your work feeling refreshed and rested. You can choose how long you want to spend doing a 'going still'. You can do a 'going still' on your own or with a group. Read through the steps and use them when you feel at ease with them.

1. In a quiet voice ask your child to close her eyes and let her hands rest naturally on her lap. You should also have your eyes closed.

2. Continue in a quiet voice, saying:

   Hear the sounds around you but take no notice of them.
   Notice your breathing going in … and out … in … and out.
   Feel the weight of your clothes on your body.
   Feel the weight of your body on the chair.
   The play of the air on your skin.

   Other appropriate phrases may come to mind, so use those. The idea is to calm down and let go of any tension by becoming focused on your body.

3. Allow a few minutes to pass – whatever feels comfortable – while you sit calmly, your bodies still, your breathing deep and relaxed.

4. After a few minutes – the longer the better – ask your child in a quiet voice to come back into the room and open her eyes.

5. Ask her how she feels now.

If you are alone and feel yourself beginning to panic about what you are working on, then simply sit still and go through the 'going still' procedure in your mind, talking yourself through each stage.

It will become an almost automatic response to stress – to still yourself and calm down.

Relaxations

The following relaxations work best if you read them out loud as your child closes her eyes, relaxes and listens. They are all calming and give your child a chance to hear soothing and comforting words while also being re-energised.

All the relaxations begin by you asking your child to close her eyes and begin breathing deeply. In a quiet voice, carry on by asking her to tighten and then relax her toes, followed by her legs and so on up the body through the bottom, stomach, chest, lower and upper back, hands, arms, shoulders, neck, face and scalp. Beginning with a tensing movement means she feels how her body is when it is relaxed because she can compare it with the sensation of tightness. By the time she has worked through her body, she will be listening in a calm way for whatever follows.

The stories all focus on something positive so you can choose which one you want to share with your child at a particular time. If she is finding it hard to make friends, for example, try the 'relaxation for playing with friends'.

A relaxation for playing with friends

Imagine for a moment that you are walking along a country lane.

It is the summer time and you can hear the birds singing and smell the scent from the flowers.

Either side of the lane are tall green hedges that are too tall for you to look over. Suddenly from behind one of the hedges you hear the sounds of children playing.

They are laughing and calling to each other.

Every so often you hear clapping and cheering and then voices shouting encouragement.

For a moment you feel lonely and left out but as you walk on you come to a gap in the hedge where there is a gate.

You lean on the gate and are able to watch the game.

There are lots of children playing. Some of them you may know, others you may not have met before.

Look at their faces and you will see they are all smiling and enjoying the game.

When someone catches the ball the others all cheer.

They are shouting to each other words of encouragement and praise.

Now watch the game they are playing and see if you can work out the rules.

As you watch they stop playing and one of the group waves at you to come and join in the game.

So you open the gate and walk through into the field.

Faces look at you and smile as someone explains to you how to play the game.

Notice how carefully you listen so that you know how to play as part of the team.

Once they are sure you are happy that you know what to do, the game starts again.

Now you are playing with everyone, catching and then throwing the ball to others.

People on your team call your name and cheer when you take part.

You hear yourself calling to other players, encouraging them and praising them.

As the afternoon wears on and the sun begins to go down, the game ends.

From somewhere some of the children bring out a picnic.

All your favourite foods are spread out and everyone flops down to have something to eat and drink.

Now you have more time to talk to your new friends.

Notice how relaxed and happy you feel, part of the group, able to join in.

You listen to others and join in the conversations.

Finally the afternoon comes to an end and it is time for you to go home.

You say good-bye to your friends and they all wave as you step back out through the gate and into the lane...

You are back now on the lane heading for home.

Notice how happy you feel as you remember the afternoon you have had, the people you have met and the game you played.

Just watch yourself strolling up the lane in the sunshine feeling positive, happy, confident and with a big smile on your face.

When you are ready you can open your eyes and sit up.

A relaxation for striving

You are standing at the foot of a very high mountain. The mountain is so high that you can't see the top. The top of the mountain is so high that it is covered by clouds.

With you at the foot of the mountain are people you know.

You tell them that you have decided to climb the mountain.

None of them think that you are going to be able to do it.

They tell you that the mountain is far too high, you'll never be able to do it, you're not strong enough.

But you know, deep inside yourself, that you can do it.

You know you can do it because you want to do it.

So, you say good-bye to the people at the bottom of the mountain and step through the little gate where the path begins that is going to take you to the top. As you walk up the gentle slopes at the foot of the mountain, notice the grass and flowers either side of the path.

The sun is warm and rabbits bound back and forwards across the path.

You feel confident and happy as you look around at the view.

As you get higher up, the path begins to get steeper. The grass becomes sparse and the slope becomes rockier. Instead of flowers, stubby little shrubs grow in the thin soil.

The air is cooler now that you are higher up. Your legs are beginning to ache and your feet to feel sore. It is difficult to breathe and you stop every now and again to get your breath.

As you climb up higher still you are in the cloud. You can feel the drops of cool moisture on your face.

You work harder and harder to scramble up the last few feet of the mountain. Notice how determined you feel to get to the top. You have come so far now and your goal is in sight.

As you reach the very top of the mountain an amazing thing happens.

The clouds part and the sun comes out.

It shines down on you and the mountain. As you flop down for a rest you realise that you can see for miles and miles. In the very far distance you can see the sea. As you look around you can see fields and forests, valleys and villages, rivers and roads so tiny that the cars on them look like toy cars.

As you look down to the bottom of the mountain you see all your friends so far away that you can't see their faces. But you can see that they are waving.

You give them a big wave, feeling proud and delighted in your own determination. It was that determination that got you up to the top. It was that determination that kept you going even when your legs were tired and your feet were sore. It was that determination that kept you going even when it would have been more comfortable and easier to stop.

When you have had a long enough rest you start to stand up. As you put your hands down to push yourself up you notice for the first time a small package in a little hollow in the rock just where you were sitting. You pick up the package and find there is a label stuck to it with your name on.

You unwrap the little package and are amazed to find inside something so perfect. Something just right for you. Something that you have always wanted.

You pop the gift into your pocket and then set off back down the mountain.

It is always easier to go down than it is to climb up and you find yourself whizzing down the rocky path. It is as though you have a sixth sense telling you just where to put your feet you are so sure footed. The path begins to level out and you are back on the grassy slopes at the foot of the mountain. Now you are really racing along jumping and skipping. You get to the little gate at the end of the path and there are all your friends.

All those people who didn't think you'd be able to do it. They are all clapping and cheering. Giving you hugs and shaking you by the hand. If you would like to you can show them your present.

Notice how happy you feel. How proud you are of having got to the top and having done it on your own. Even when other people doubted that you could do it you were determined to do it for yourself.

Just stay there for a moment surrounded by your friends, feeling confident.

Then when you are ready you can open your eyes and come back to your surroundings.

A relaxation for feeling calm

It is a warm summer afternoon and you are strolling along a path which winds around the side of a mountain. You can hear birds singing and are enjoying the view.

After a few minutes you come to a cave in the side of the hill. The cave feels safe and inviting so you step inside. At first you can't see very much at all but as your eyes become accustomed to the darkness you are able to make out precious stones; rubies, diamonds and emeralds, glittering in the walls of the cave.

You walk deeper into the cave fascinated by the gems and the stalactites that hang from the roof and the stalagmites that are growing up from the floor. The path takes you deeper into the cave. As you walk you feel a calm air settling over you. In the distance you can hear the rumblings and grumblings of the earth but they are far off and do not worry you.

Eventually you come to an enormous underground cavern lit by the glittering of all the jewels and tiny rays of sunlight which have worked their way in through cracks and fissures in the earth.

In the centre of the cavern is a huge underground lake. The surface is so smooth it looks like black glass. As you stand and watch the lake and hear the waves gently lapping on the shore you feel peaceful and serene. The still and quiet lake seems to be a reflection of your feelings.

While you watch, a flock of swans of all different colours, blues, greens and golds, swim gently towards you. They glide across the still surface of the lake hardly causing a ripple.

Walk round the edge of the lake until you come to an old person sitting and looking at the water.

The old person turns to you and smiles as you approach, and invites you to sit down.

For a few moments the two of you sit side by side gazing at the water and listening to the gentle noises.

The old person begins to speak and explains to you that the lake is a point of stillness in the centre of the earth.

You ask if you are allowed to come back and visit the lake. The old person replies that any time you want to you can visit your own lake of stillness which you have inside you. All that you need to do is close your eyes and go still and you will find you have your own lake of stillness.

Finally, the old person gives you a precious gem to remind you of your visit. Look at the gem for a moment and then put it away safely in your pocket.

Now you are ready to return to the outside world. You follow the path as it winds its way back past the stalagmites and stalactites and towards the sunlight and the side of the mountain. Notice how calm and relaxed you feel, how confident and purposeful.

Finally you reach the entrance to the cave.

The sunlight welcomes you back to the warm summer afternoon. You touch the gem which is safe in your pocket and remember your special visit to the stillness at the centre of the earth.

Just lie there for a few moments feeling warm, relaxed and calm.

When you are ready you can open your eyes and return to the room.

A relaxation for feeling loved

It is a warm sunny day in the summer and you are walking along a path which is at the bottom of a valley.

As you look from side to side you can see the slopes of the mountains around you and as you look up you can see the point where they meet the sky.

The path you are walking along is at the side of a river. As you walk you can hear the water gurgling over the rocks. You can hear birds singing and can smell the fresh grass and flowers.

Look to the top of one of the hills and you see a figure silhouetted against the skyline. The figure looks familiar. As you watch, the figure moves down from the top of the mountain towards you. You watch the figure closely and realise that you do know who it is. It may be someone that you haven't seen for a very long time. You find a path that will take you up to meet them as they walk down. As you walk towards each other you feel excited at the prospect of meeting this old friend. Someone who knew you a long time ago. Someone you love and someone who loves you.

Finally you meet. You may hug or smile, you might start talking straight away. Whatever happens, notice your happiness at meeting up with this person. This person who you feel knows who you are. Now you both walk together along the path. You tell your friend about what has been happening to you and your loved friend reminds you of times that you spent together. Your friemd tells you how much you are cared for. This special person tells you how proud people are of what you have done.

You walk along full of a sense of pride, full of loving thoughts and feelings. It is so lovely to know that you are special to this person.

Finally your friend says that it is time to go. You say good-bye and both of you go back the way you came, turning to wave until you disappear from each other's sight.

But instead of feeling lonely now that your friend has gone, you feel surrounded and protected by your friend's love.

You know that whenever you want you can close your eyes and meet up with your special friend on the path.

As you walk back the way you came, notice how calm and peaceful you feel. Remember that there are people in your life who you may not see very often but who care about you and are proud of your achievements and who love you because you are you.

When you are ready, open your eyes and sit calmly.

A relaxation for building confidence

Begin by looking directly ahead at a fixed point, without blinking, for three seconds. Then close your eyes.

Breathe in and then out, breathe in and then out.

Continue the counting through until the child is breathing in a relaxed and steady way. If the child is unsettled, it may calm them to work through the body, tightening and relaxing different areas.

Imagine that you are on a rough and choppy sea in a small boat. You have been cast off from the cruiser that you were on. The waves buffet the boat, causing it to rock violently, and you know that sooner or later the boat is going to be tipped over. Suddenly, a huge frightening wave hits the side of the boat flipping it into the air and over into the water. You go under almost immediately coughing and spluttering.

To your amazement however, in this magical world you can breathe under water. There is a stillness and a calm below the crashing waves above. Around you the water is enveloping you protectively and you sink effortlessly into the black depths below.

You breathe gently under the water, in... and out ... in ... and out, sinking slowly. Around you swim fish, dolphins, sharks, but none of them seem concerned by your presence.

The darkness soon surrounds you totally with only an occasional pinprick of light from those special fish that make their own light on the ocean floor. You have reached the end of your descent, and there on the ocean floor is a cave.

You swim into the cave – confident that it is a place of safety.

Here you can vary the relaxation.

1. *In the cave you see a picture of yourself doing something very well. Look at the detail in the picture – how you are standing or sitting, the expression on your face, the colours, how confidently you are doing the activity.*

2. *In the cave is the thing you most want.*

3. *In the cave are people you love who are all pleased to see you. They are delighted that you have come so far to be with them. You move around the cave talking and being with different people. You share each other's stories and hear people remembering times gone by and planning what to do in the future.*

When you have finished you slowly swim back up to the calm surface, remembering the in... and out... breathing pattern. When you reach the surface you can sit up, open your eyes and wait for the others.

A relaxation for being adventurous

See yourself walking down a path that meanders along next to a river.

It is a warm and sunny day.

You notice what the path is made from – it may be stones, sand or earth trodden hard by the many people that have walked that way.

The sun glints through the trees which grow down to the water's edge and cast shadows across the path.

You are enjoying the walk, the sun and the trees.

Suddenly, something catches your eye on the opposite bank.

Looking across you see a hot air balloon, inflated and just ready for take off.

In the basket under the balloon you can see the travellers, excited and eager to be off.

As you watch, you imagine what fun it must be to ride in an air balloon and you wish that you too were on the other side of the river and could have a go.

But on your side you only have the trees, the sun and the path.

Continuing on with your walk once again, your attention is drawn to the far bank where this time you see a field of graceful white horses. There are people in the field too. Some of them are feeding and stroking the horses while others are getting ready to go off on a ride. As you watch, you imagine what fun it would be to be over there in the field and you wish that you could ride one of the white horses too.

You carry on walking along the path. The sun is still warm and the path continues through the trees and by the water.

As you look over the river again you see a fairground on the other side. There are big wheels and stalls, rides and games. People are walking around enjoying the fair. You wish that you could get to the fair. Everyone looks happy and seems to be enjoying the stalls and rides but there doesn't seem any way that you can get across to join them.

Suddenly you round a bend in the river and there ahead you see an old and very rickety wooden bridge. It doesn't look like it has been used for a long time but it does stretch across the river and would mean that you could get across to the other side.

As you approach the bridge you see that it is old and you wonder whether it is strong enough to support you. But as you carefully put your foot on to the bridge you discover to your amazement that it is actually quite secure. Instead of it being wobbly and unstable it feels firm and safe. In fact there doesn't seem any difference between the path and the bridge.

In a few seconds you are on the other side. Now you can race back to the fair or the horses or the hot air balloon.

You spend a lovely afternoon enjoying everything on that side of the river. You float over the countryside in the basket under the balloon, you ride across fields on one of the beautiful white horses and you have a go on the rides at the fair. Time whizzes past with you enjoying every minute.

At the end of the afternoon you get back home across the bridge.

And now you know where the bridge is you can get across to the other side of the river whenever you want.

When you are ready you can open your eyes and sit up.

A relaxation for concentration

Imagine that you are sitting on a rock that juts out into the sea.

It is a warm and sunny day.

As you look down at the water you see the sun glinting off its surface making it shimmer and glisten, dazzling you with its sparkle.

Carry on looking at the water and gradually you will be able to see more than the glittering surface. You begin to see fish swimming around. Fish that are bright colours, pinks and greens, blues and yellows.

As your eyes become used to the fish you notice the green fronds of seaweed drifting back and forth in the water, being carried by the tide. Sometimes the seaweed covers up the fish and sometimes the seaweed drifts away and you can see them.

Every now and again as you look into the water you catch a glimpse of bright colours right at the bottom of the sea. Because of all the movement, the glinting of the sun, the fish and the fronds of seaweed it's difficult to make out what the new colours are. No matter how hard you try to look, it's impossible to tell what is down there until a dolphin swims up to you from the depths. He comes up to the rock and beckons you to join him. You drop down onto his back and begin a magical journey into the sea. You find you can breathe under the water as he carries you down past the fishes and the seaweed to the very bottom of the sea.

Once you are there you can see what it was making the colours, for there on the floor of the sea is a most beautiful mosaic made out of tiny, colourful shells. They have all been placed together to make swirling and whirling patterns. It's like looking through a kaleidoscope. You swim across the mosaic looking at all the sections and taking in the patterns.

The dolphin appears and gives you a tiny shell which you decide to add to the mosaic. Carefully you look for a space where you can fit your shell and once you find one you place your shell into the pattern.

The dolphin appears again and as you climb on his back he whisks you back up to the rock where your adventure began.

As you climb back onto the rock you look down into the water. You can still see the fish and the green fronds but now you know what is there on the sea bed. In your mind's eye you have a picture of a wonderful pattern that you helped to make.

When you are ready you can open your eyes and sit up.

A relaxation for feeling more positive

Imagine that you have discovered a secret door in your house. You have never noticed this door before – it may look exactly like the rest of the wall or it may have been behind a curtain or a piece of furniture.

You try the door to see whether it is unlocked and find that you can open it. As you step through the doorway you find yourself in an empty, white room. The floor is white, the walls are white and the ceiling is white.

Then you notice in the middle of the floor a white, wooden table. On the top of the table is a beautiful bowl. It is the only colourful thing in the room. The pattern on the bowl seems to light up the whole room. The colours on the bowl are rich and jewel like.

You walk towards the bowl wondering what could be inside.

As you look in you see that it is filled with exotic fruits. Fruit you love and new fruits you have never tasted.

And there right on the top of this luscious pile of fruit is a beautiful, large orange. It seems to be glowing like a golden sun.

You pick up the orange and feel a tingling sensation trickle up your arm.

You begin to peel the orange becoming excited at what is going to be inside this magnificent piece of fruit.

And then you discover what it is – a large and precious jewel nestling in the peel.

You notice the colour of the jewel and the weight and touch of it in your hand. You feel amazed and proud of your discovery.

Holding onto the jewel you leave the room...

When you are ready you can open your eyes.

A relaxation for knowing you can learn

Close your eyes and think of something you're really good at now. Now think about what you were like a year ago.

What have you learnt in the last year?

Think about next year.

What do you hope you will be able to do next year that you can't do now?

Think again about what you're good at now and think of what you did that made you as good as this.

Just notice all the little things you had to learn to be so clever at it.

When you are ready, open your eyes.

Turning can't do into can do

The relaxation begins with you asking your child to think of something she feels really good at. This is often difficult for someone who feels hopeless at everything. If your child is having trouble, remind her of something you think she is good at. It can be anything – watching television, sport, being kind to others – any activity you feel your child is good at, even if others see it as unusual. Now ask your child to think of the thing she is wanting to change. Once you have established these 'positive and negative pictures', begin the relaxation.

Sit quietly with your hands on your lap and your eyes closed. Now tense and relax your body one bit at time. Start with your toes – tense and relax, then your feet, lower leg, knees, upper leg, bottom, lower back, shoulders, scalp, face, chest, stomach, upper arms, elbows, lower arms and finally scrunch your fingers into a ball and then let the fingers wriggle and relax.

(This tensing and relaxing of individual parts of the body will help you prepare for the next step.)

Now make a picture in your mind of the activity or memory you feel positive about. Notice how you are moving in that picture- the colours, sounds, shapes, smells, sights, and textures which are part of the picture.

Now change the positive picture to the negative and notice the detail in this one. How are the colours, sounds, shapes and so on here?

Change the picture to the positive one and notice this time how you are moving, the expression on your face, what your thoughts are.

Go back to the picture which makes you feel stressful. This time only stay with that picture briefly looking at the colours and your expression and how you are moving.

Return to the picture where you feel relaxed and in control. Notice how you think while you are doing this activity; how you plan to make sure you get maximum enjoyment, how you feel when you make a mistake, how you see a mistake as an opportunity to learn, how you will think about the activity when you have finished it.

Cast your mind to the picture of the activity that makes you feel you are failing. Notice how you feel about a mistake here.

Go back into the good picture. This time vary all the bits of it. Change the colour, the shapes, the sounds – play with it. It is your picture. Finally bring all the bits back to be just how you want them.

For the last time, go into the weak picture. It may have faded and if it has disappeared just let it go, but if there are any bits left let them fall to the floor. By you is a dustpan and brush. Sweep up the pieces and you will see a bin with a tight fitting lid. Put them in and put on the lid.

Finally go back into the picture of the thing that makes you feel confident, happy, sure of yourself and your position in the world – and when you are ready, open your eyes.

Foot massage

The foot massage technique can be used to relax and calm. It is best done on bare feet.

Your child sits comfortably on a chair with feet resting on your lap.

Begin by squeezing the big toe at the top and base of the toe nail.

This releases tension and can be repeated at intervals throughout the massage.

Then, using small circular motions, gently circle along the bones on the top of the foot.

It is important that you wash your hands in cold water after the massage. This is to release the tension that you will have picked up during the massage. If you forget, you will find that you feel very tired as you are carrying around someone else's tension.

Simply stretch

Just a quick stretch can work wonders!

Stand up and put your arms straight out in front of you. Now give yourself a really tight hug – a real bone crusher.

Stretch your arms out straight again and this time bring them round to behind your back in wide circles. Try doing it three times!

GOOD  LUCK